Another Way

Recent Poetry from Lamar University Literary Press

Bobby Aldridge, *An Affair of the Stilled Heart*
Walter Bargen, *My Other Mother's Red Mercedes*
Charles Behlen, *Failing Heaven*
Jerry Bradley, *Collapsing into Possibility*
Mark Busby, *Through Our Times*
Julie Chappell, *Mad Habits of a Life*
Stan Crawford, *Resisting Gravity*
Glover Davis, *My Cap of Darkness*
William Virgil Davis, *The Bones Poems*
Jeffrey DeLotto, *Voices Writ in Sand*
Chris Ellery, *Elder Tree*
Dede Fox, *On Wings of Silence*
Alan Gann, *That's Entertainment*
Larry Griffin, *Cedar Plums*
Michelle Hartman, *Irony and Irrelevance*
Katherine Hoerth, *Goddess Wears Cowboy Boots*
Michael Jennings, *Crossings: A Record of Travel*
Gretchen Johnson, *A Trip Through Downer, Minnesota*
Ulf Kirchdorfer, *Hamlet in Exhile*
Jim McGarrah, *A Balancing Act*
J. Pittman McGehee, *Nod of Knowing*
Erin Murphy, *Ancilla*
John Milkereit, *Drive the World in a Taxicab*
Laurence Musgrove, *A Stranger's Heart*
Benjamin Myers, *The Family Book of Martyrs*
Janice Northerns, *Some Electric Hum*
Godspower Oboido, *Wandering Feet on Pebbled Shores*
Carol Coffee Reposa, *Sailing West*
Jan Seale, *Elder Skelter*
Steven Schroeder, *the moon, not the finger, pointing*
Glen Sorestad, *Hazards of Eden*
Vincent Spina, *The Sumptuous Hills of Gulfport*
W.K. Stratton, *Betrayal Creek*
Wally Swist, *Invocation*
Ken Waldman, *Sports Page*
Loretta Diane Walker, *Ode to My Mother's Voice*
Dan Williams, *Past Purgatory, a Distant Paradise*
Jonas Zdanys, *Three White Horses*

For information on these and other Lamar University Literary
Press books go to www.Lamar.edu/literarypress

Another Way

Poetry and Prose by High School Students in Jefferson County, Texas

Edited by Kate Williams

LITERARY PRESS
LAMAR UNIVERSITY

ISBN: 978-1-962148-12-2
Library of Congress Control Number: 2024945387

Cover Design: Rachel Guthrie

Lamar University Literary Press
Beaumont, Texas

CONTENTS

9	Introduction by Kate Williams
13	Indian Ocean Tsunami by Jazmin Almaguer
15	Climate Controlled Prejudice by Marlene Alvarez
16	The Mysterious Ghosty Hurricane by Jennifer Arredondo
19	Extreme Weather & Inequality by Maryah Barragan
21	Untitled by Monica Becerra
23	Decimation by Jenna Bleakley
24	Extreme Weather and Inequality by Brenya Boudreaux
25	Untitled by Brianna Brottem
26	Untitled by Hannah Campbell
27	Extreme Weather and Inequality: Bridging the Gap for a Resilient Future by Lola Carr
31	Life Turned Upside Down by Victoria Ceja
33	My Little Dog by Ashley Collins
34	Nature's Temper by Eve Winters Compton
35	Nature's Fury by Guadalupe Contreras Bernabe
37	Extreme Weather and Inequality: A Closer Look at the Connection by Angela Cooley
39	Untitled by Brady Corcoran
41	How Did I Get Here? by Marshalei' Daniels
43	Life After Ike by Tacota Deiss
48	Survivor by Raul A. Diaz
50	Changes by Jasmine Do
52	Navigating the Storm by Kayde Dotson
53	25,360 Years by Kowen Ducote
55	Weather and Inequality by Emma Ferguson
57	Untitled by Emily Flores
59	Rising Waters, Deep Divides: Unraveling the Systemic Issues of Weather Inequality by Horacio Garcia
62	Extreme Weather & Inequality by Kimora Garrett
64	Within The Eye of The Storm by Alyssa Garsea
66	Natural Disasters by Gabriella Haley
67	My Love, Mostly Hate Relationship with Hurricanes by Olivia Harms
69	The Hurricane That Changed Lives by Colby Harrington
71	Another Way by Sakara Harris
73	2023 Climate Crisis by Syndi Hatchel
75	Extreme Weather & Inequality by Deacon Hebert
77	Untitled by Scott Lucian Helt

79	Untitled by Larissa Heniger
80	Untitled by Erin Hollier
82	The Connection by Christopher Johnson
83	Untitled by Aletra Jones
84	Untitled by Jael Jones
85	Equity in the Eye of the Storm: The Impact of Extreme Weather on Vulnerable Communities by Ibrahim Khankhail
86	Blown Around in the Wind by Marissa Lang
88	Untitled by Aiden Le
90	Extreme Weather & Inequality by Ayonna Lewis
92	Our Journey Towards Resolving Extreme Weather Inequalities by Crystal Liu
95	Screams by Abril Lopez
96	Climas Extremos y Desigualdad/Extreme Weather and Inequality por/by Adithleidy Lopez-Magallon
99	Tyler's Storm by Matthew Lou
103	A Story of Hurricanes, Trailer Parks, and Hope by Jamie Lyles
106	Summer Dies in December by Olivia de la Madrid
107	Extreme Weather and Inequality by Ryan Makelki
110	Surviving Hurricane Harvey: A Ten-Year-Old's Perspective by Leydi Mariel Mascareno
113	Inequality and Extreme Weather Events by Joshua Mendoza
117	Untitled by Mason Miller
119	The Sun Does Not Always Symbolize Happiness by Ilahi Modh
121	Mother Nature's Wrath by Camren Nichols
124	Untitled by Gabrielle Owens
125	Extreme Weather and Inequality by Parth Patel
126	Thunder and Storms by Kennedy Perkins
127	Untitled by baile randle
129	Ancient to the Future Project by Brady Redding
132	Drowning by Arismel Reyes
135	Lake of Memories by Reagan Rigby
139	Interstellar Justice Seeker by Armajah Robinson
142	Togetherness by Lexcey Savoy
145	Untitled by Christian Shaw
147	Does History Really Change? by Teigan Smith
149	Letters of My World's End by Aiden Sowell
152	The Winter Storm by Avery Spell

153   Extreme Weather and Inequality: A Looming Crisis by Holden Stucker

155   Extreme Weather in the Twin Islands of the Caribbean by Georgia Thomson

157   The Storm That Changed Everything by Abygail Valentine

161   Not Flooded by Brady Vo

164   Extreme Weather vs. Inequality by Joshua A. Wilson

166   The Hurricanc by Emily Xu

167   Untitled by Molly Young

168   Lovely Weather by Treyquinn Young

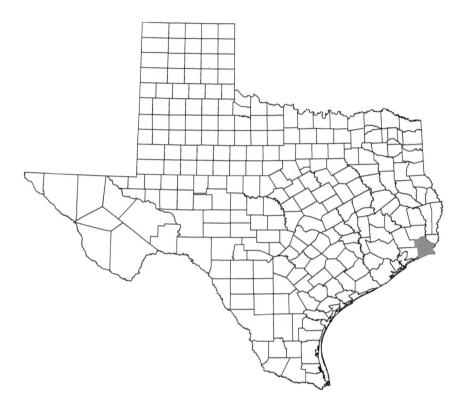

Jefferson County is in Southeast Texas on the Gulf of Mexico. Map by David Benbennick. Public domain.

https://commons.wikimedia.org/w/index.php?curid=573186

Introduction

by Kate Williams

The writings here resulted from a Fall 2023 contest for the best writing on Extreme Weather and Inequality. Writers had to be attending one of the five biggest high schools in Jefferson County, Texas. One student from each school was awarded $5,000, and two more won "special mention" prizes of $1,000. The five are Lola Carr (Beaumont United High School), Crystal Liu (West Brook), Jamie Lyles (Port Neches-Groves), Leydi Mariel Mascareno (Memorial), and Camren Nichols (Nederland); and the two are Sakara Harris (West Brook) and Adithleidy Lopez-Magallon (Nederland). Their poems, essays, or stories are joined here by sixty-nine others, all worth reading.

Why? How? What can happen next?

A public conversation took place at Lamar University in 2022. Twenty plus people from across the county spoke about two linked and persistent issues: Inequality and Extreme Weather. Rational dialogue and good ideas flowed. People met for the first time. All this was remarkable in the context. A second event soon took shape. Both events were videorecorded, so you can watch them online at http://ancienttothefuture.org. The first event was published in the Beaumont Enterprise and the Texas Gulf Historical and Biographical Record. Then, since all the participants were college age or older, the contest was invented expressly to get young people's thoughts and ideas.

Jefferson County is in southeast Texas, on the Gulf of Mexico close to Louisiana. It sees the highest summer "feels-like" temps, the biggest storms, the heaviest rains, the highest pollution and health impacts. Since oil first gushed out of the ground here in 1901, Jefferson County has maintained an economic focus on oil, gas, and chemicals—making and storing, transporting and exporting. Those industries keep a lid on frank discussion because their bottom lines depend on a continual flow of fossil fuel. Yet even these companies have had to make at least gestures in the direction of change.

The county has also become more Black and Brown over the last 100 years. Beaumont, the biggest city, was already one-third African American in 1890, having been a refuge from the plantations and offering jobs in lumber and cattle. (Today it is at roughly one-half African American.) Soon Port Arthur was attracting Mexican and other Spanish speaking people to jobs in the oil and gas; today Latinos are the largest part of that city. Other smaller cities have seen inbound white flight. The county is also poorer than elsewhere in Texas, but that poverty is unequally spread across the area. It includes the two most unionized zip codes in Texas, 77627 in Nederland and number two, 77619 in Groves.

The sponsor of the Lamar meetings and the contest, was the Ancient to the Future Project, founded by a child of Beaumont, Dave Williams, and me, his older daughter. Our goal has been to foster democratic dialogue on stubborn social issues, towards solutions. Our campus hosts, the Center for History and Culture of Southeast Texas and the Upper Gulf Coast and the Department of Sociology, Social Work, and Criminal Justice, help make all this possible.

The writing contest attracted interest from students as well as principals, teachers, and school staff. Writing began to come in. Out of the organizing, a team of local judges was assembled.

In the middle of this, ChatGPT went mainstream. We had to acknowledge that clever—or even not so clever—use of AI helped create some submissions. It is near impossible to tell. We decided that any future contests would have to include an oral component. If you can't say it out loud, you probably didn't write it. Our own experiments with ChatGPT told us we are at the beginning of something strange and new. But for now, we opted for and encouraged local content—one of the weaknesses of AI.

So most of the writings here are emphatically local. What is more, a great many of them tell the harrowing and personal stories of Hurricane Harvey and its aftermath. Seven years ago, this storm dumped five feet of rain over five days. The water had nowhere to go. Buildings began to rot in the wet. People were stranded. At the time, these high school student authors were in elementary school. So this book is a record of what it was really like for a child to survive that storm.

It is also testament to the global awareness of these young writers. You can read about weather disasters in Trinidad and Tobago ... Bangladesh ... the 2004 Indian Ocean tsunami ... and other international and US locations. You can read speculative fiction about other planets, works that are representative of the newest genre: cli-fi.

Speaking from so much experience, and careful reflection, this book is a call to face extreme weather and inequality *Another Way*. Sakara Harris's poem later in this book gives us the title. Many writers here share her thoughts and feelings.

As the book was in production, extreme rain and flooding—and a lot of houses are built on floodplains—caused the local paper to assure people it wasn't another Harvey. People in this county are jittery about hurricanes every year from May to November.

We hope this book is itself *Another Way* to help heal and prevent the injuries and traumas of extreme weather and inequality. These writers have earned our respect. We urge you to read and respond in any way you can.

Indian Ocean Tsunami
by Jazmin Almaguer

At 7:59 am of December 26, 2004, the world witnessed one of the deadliest tsunamis recorded in history. The Indian Ocean tsunami. Triggered by a 9.1 magnitude quake off the coast of Sumatra and Indonesia. The tsunami topped 100 feet and traveled across the Indian Ocean at about 500 mph. It had claimed about 230,000 thousand lives. It came as a shock since no one had the time to prepare what would happen. In this introduction, we will dive into the causes, consequences, and global response to the Indian Ocean tsunami. Trying to shed some light on the toll and impact it had on the community.

It started with an earthquake so bad it spiked up to 9.1 magnitude. It was so bad that the earthquake stands as the third largest earthquake to be ever recorded since 1900. It was about 30 kilometers deep and 1,300 kilometers wide. Indonesia, Bangladesh, India, Malaysia, the Maldives, Myanmar, Singapore, Sri Lanka, and Thailand all felt the shaking but the damage and casualties was mostly caused in India and Indonesia. The tsunami hit Indonesia within twenty minutes and it hit Africa seven hours later. The waves reached 51 meters and flooded inland about 5 kilometers. The tsunami itself impacted seventeen countries and roughly killed a quarter million people who were either missing or presumed dead.

Nearly about 1.7 million people were displaced. The total damages came to about 13 billion dollars. Indonesia nearly lost about 6 billion dollars in damages. There was no warning or alert to be spread since the cell towers were damaged. Only a text went through but only so many got it after the internet was damaged. No sirens were able to play throughout the countries. The authorities are also at fault since they have been accused of canceling the alert too soon. No one was prepared to leave or had the time to think about what their next move was.

If a tsunami warning was ever sent out in time then casualties would be much less severe. It would have saved thousands of lives and less damage. There was a system in place at that time but never used. Now that the 2004 tsunami hit the Indian Ocean it highlighted the reality of a tsunami hit. It has raised global awareness all across the pacific ocean. The Indian Ocean Tsunami Warning and Mitigation System, which is led by Australia, India, and Indonesia has been placed so now they get text messages, assess threats and issues that come up.

Works Cited

Dawson, Sue. "Indonesia Tsunami: Why Wasn't There an Earlier Warning?" *The Conversation,* 31 Jan. 2023, theconver
sation.com/indonesia-tsunami-why-wasnt-there-an-ear
lier-warning-104265#:~:text=The%20Indonesian%20au
thorities%20in%20this,cancelling%20the%20warning%20
too%20soon.

*Jetstream Max: 2004 Indian Ocean Tsunami | National Oceanic
And ...,* 12 June 2023, www.noaa.gov/jetstream/2004tsu_
max.

Reid, Kathryn. "2004 Indian Ocean Earthquake and Tsunami:
Facts, Faqs, How to Help." *World Vision,* 25 Sept. 2023,
www.worldvision.org/disaster-relief-news-sto
ries/2004-indian-ocean-earthquake-tsunami-facts#:~:
text=In%20Banda%20Aceh%2C%20the%20landmass,
speed%20of%20a%20jet%20plane.

Climate Controlled Prejudice
by Marlene Alvarez

Living in Southeast Texas means dealing with the harsh weather conditions. When a national disaster like this does occur, it's devastating for the residence dealing with the aftermath. People who are considered lower class have the short end of the stick when it comes to thcsc situations, and getting government assistance.

Hurricane season begins typically from around the beginning of June to late November. Over the years we have experienced a few catastrophic storms, including Hurricane Harvey. This category 4 storm caused so much damage and even took some lives. It was a good example of how bad tropical storms could get at this time of year. It left an impact on Texans, and made us better equipped for the next time something like this could happen.

After the storm many neighborhoods were affected, some houses flooded, and some were destroyed altogether. People were offered resources from the government such as care packages, food, and money. FEMA, or Federal Emergency Management Agency, began to give funds to people who needed it. Quoting www.pbs.org, FEMA aid disproportionately went to more wealthier folks rather than lower middle class people who needed it the most. It's a common occurrence for upper class families to receive a lot more than people of a lower class. This undoubtedly made it much harder for working class families to get back on their feet.

The repercussions of natural disasters puts everyone dealing with it in a vulnerable state, especially people with low income housing. Hurricanes have left people homeless, without a job, or school. I have experienced a devastating hurricane first hand, and it flooded my home and most of my belongings. School was also shut down for me, so I had to go to a new one. It distressed people in different ways and put them in a bad situation.

Considering all this, harsh weather conditions and national disasters are devastating times for the people who deal with them. Lower income people however, have it the hardest and are more susceptible to being treated unfairly.

The Mysterious Ghosty Hurricane
by Jennifer Arredondo

"Everyone, hide and protect yourselves; we are in a state of emergency!" said the authorities. Everything changed after that warning message. My name is Flor, and forty years ago, I was an average high school student in her senior year, living an everyday life, until a strange event happened that changed my life. I lived with my grandparents, Pipo and Mima, on Flora Island in the Caribbean Sea. Pipo and Mima have cared for me since I was three. My parents disappeared on my third birthday, leaving me at my grandparents' house. Nobody heard of them since that day. It was a mystery I didn't want to solve, or at least that is what I thought.

Thursday, May 19, 1983, I was walking back home from school with my best friend Lia when suddenly I noticed the sky turning gray and a massive cloud forming in the center. "We should hurry up; it seems like it's going to rain," said Lia. Twenty minutes later, I was sitting with Mima on the front porch cutting fruits, and suddenly, it started to heavily rain with strong winds that made all the leaves fall as if we were in autumn. All you could hear were the mad thunders. "That's weird. I didn't hear anything about a storm in the news, plus it is not storm season," said Mima. Pipo looked worried and said, "The authorities launched an emergency alert asking people to find a safe hiding place. They say something weird is happening, but the radars can't identify it." Mima quickly stood up. "I am not staying out here any longer; let's go inside," said Grandma. I had mixed feelings about this storm: I was scared, and at the same time, I wasn't. Minutes and hours passed, and the weather didn't get any better. The power went out, trees had fallen over, and roads were impassable. All we had was an old radio to listen to the news. Meteorologists were working to identify this mysterious storm and where it came from.

Constant rain, winds, and thunders lasted for five days in a row. Still, radars couldn't see or identify the storm. Meteorologists defined it as a hurricane because it had all the features of one, but it was unique because it was undetectable. That is how it got the name of "Ghosty hurricane." On Wednesday, when the tempest was gone, everyone on the island started to clean and recover from the devastating hurricane. I still had mixed feelings; for some reason, the only thing I could think about during the storm was my parents. I was unsure what they had to do with all this chaos, but I was determined to find out.

According to meteorologists, the storm was classified as a category three hurricane, with speed winds of one hundred and fifteen miles per hour. It killed three thousand people with its pass. Even though the island has suffered from other storms due to its location, none were as catastrophic as Ghosty. Some areas of the island were impossible to go to. Rescuers had difficulty trying to rescue the victims who were under debris. The bright island was dark, and its loving people were sad. Even though the storm already passed by, the gray clouds were still part of the landscape. Nevertheless, little by little, Flora and its inhabitants started to recover. The sun rose, and with it, hope.

Out of nowhere, and as if by magic, the deadly hurricane returned. "Everyone, hide and protect yourselves; we are in a state of emergency!" said the authorities. I ran as fast as I could to get to the house quickly. When I entered, I could only see Mima. Pipo was nowhere to be found. "I need to go out and look for him," I said. "NO! You can't; it's too dangerous outside. I can't lose you too like I lost your dad," Mima said, crying, but instantly covered her mouth.

"Mima, what are you saying? What happened to my dad?" Mima just stared at me without saying a word. Just as I was about to ask her again, I heard the door. I turned around, and there was Pipo. I ran to him while crying, "Pipo, where were you? You scared me." Pipo smiled and said, "My little girl, don't worry, I was just getting some batteries and water from the convenience store. Besides, I'm old but strong," he laughed. I sighed in relief, determined to investigate what Mima hid from me.

"David, the storm chaser, was flying his plane for a new adventure when he noticed Ghosty returning towards Flora. Immediately, David contacted the authorities. A&G News' meteorologists traced the path of Ghosty. It's believed that it did not disappear but continued to the Caribbean Sea, south of the island, where it made its turn. It's predicted to touch land as a category 4 hurricane with speed winds of one hundred and forty-five miles per hour and maximum sustained wind gusts of one hundred and sixty miles per hour. The government declared a state of cyclonic alarm. Once again, please stay safe. I'm Monica Miranda, A&G News." Pipo turned off the radio.

"I'm going to take a nap. Let me know if they say anything else in the news," I told Pipo and Mima. I went to my room, but I had other plans. There was a door that divided my grandparents' and my room. I quietly went into their room. I needed to find the truth about my parents. I started to get impatient as I looked everywhere but couldn't find anything. I gave up and sat on the closet's floor when I noticed a false floor tile under Mima's shoe organizer.

Hope returned to my soul. I lifted the tile and found a wooden box. I gasped as I opened it. I couldn't believe what my eyes were seeing.

"Mima, what is this? Don't lie to me anymore. I beg you to tell me the truth," I said with tears in my eyes. Mima and Pipo approached me, held my hand, and asked me to sit. "Your dad was a storm chaser; he loved his job. One day, he came to us holding the hand of a beautiful girl, whom he introduced as his girlfriend. We were happy for him; they seemed to love each other. Four years later, you were born. We were getting ready for your third birthday when a strange meteorological event suddenly occurred. Your mom was scared, she gave me a letter and made me promise that I would protect you with my life. After that, I never saw them ever again. I never told you because I wanted to protect you," said Mima with tears rolling down her chin. "What did the letter say? Why is it not here in the box? All I see are pictures of my parents and these newspaper cutouts about a deadly storm." Mima couldn't talk, so Pipo continued for her, "In that letter, your mom told us a secret that we couldn't believe. It took us until now to understand that she was telling the truth. Your mom is The Princess Bloom of Blossom Kingdom." "What? I have never heard of that Kingdom." I said with a confused look on my face. Grandpa continues, "It doesn't belong in this universe. There is life out of the Milky Way, and your mom is proof of it. Her Kingdom captured her and your dad after she escaped from them. She didn't want to become the queen." Suddenly, the rain and thunder stopped as if the storm disappeared. The front door opened, and a bright light came into the room. Two people stood at the entrance, and one said, "My little princess, we are back, and we will stay forever." I couldn't believe it. "Mom? Dad?"

The same storm that took my parents from me brought them back. My mom fought for her freedom, and I am proud of her. Although it caused damage, I thank Ghosty for getting my parents back.

Extreme Weather & Inequality
by Maryah Barragan

Hurricane Harvey made a huge impact on Texas. This powerful hurricane hit in 2017 and was one of the costliest natural disasters in U.S. history. It made landfall in Texas as a Category 4 hurricane, bringing intense winds and record-breaking rainfall. The storm caused widespread flooding and destruction, particularly in the Houston metropolitan area. Thousands of homes were damaged or destroyed, and many communities were left devastated. The response efforts from both local and national organizations were massive, with volunteers and first responders working tirelessly to rescue and provide support to those affected. The resilience and strength of the people of Texas were truly remarkable during this challenging time.

When it comes to the inequality in Texas during Hurricane Harvey, it was a tough situation for many people. Low-income communities and marginalized groups were hit the hardest, as they often have limited resources and access to insurance. This made it even more difficult for them to recover from the damage caused by the hurricane. The inequalities that already existed in these communities were further magnified during this challenging time.

Many low-income neighborhoods lacked the necessary resources and infrastructure to withstand the powerful forces of the storm. Their homes, often located in areas prone to flooding, were severely damaged or destroyed, leaving families displaced and without a place to call home. Additionally, these communities faced limited access to insurance, making it even more difficult for them to recover and rebuild their lives. The economic impact on low-income residents was significant, as many lost their jobs due to business closures and disruptions in the local economy. The lack of financial resources further hindered their ability to recover and meet their basic needs. Moreover, the already existing inequalities in education and healthcare were amplified, as schools and healthcare facilities in these areas were severely affected, leaving residents with limited access to essential services. It is crucial to recognize and address these disparities to ensure that all communities, regardless of income level, have the support and resources needed to recover from natural disasters. These communities often faced unique challenges and vulnerabilities that made them more susceptible to the destructive forces of the hurricane. Many of the homes in these areas were not built to withstand such a powerful storm, resulting in severe damage or complete destruction. Families were left displaced and without a place to call home. It is crucial to recognize the disparities that exist and address them in order to ensure that all communities, regardless of their income level, have the necessary support and resources to recover from natural disasters. By providing equal opportunities for recovery and rebuilding, we can work towards creating a more equitable society.

Many families have relied on assistance from government programs, non-profit organizations, and community support to address their immediate needs. They have been working hard to repair and rebuild their damaged homes, seeking financial aid and grants to cover the costs. Additionally, families have been collaborating with insurance companies to file claims and receive compensation for their losses. Some families have also taken advantage of low-interest loans to help with the recovery process. Community support has played a crucial role, with neighbors helping each other with cleanup, repairs, and emotional support. Families have been resilient, adapting to new circumstances and finding ways to move forward. They have been leaning on each other for emotional support and seeking counseling services to cope with the trauma caused by the hurricane. Schools and educational institutions have been working diligently to provide resources and support to students and families affected by the disaster. It's inspiring to see the strength and determination of these families as they navigate the recovery process. It's important for us to recognize these disparities and work towards creating a more equitable society, where everyone has equal opportunities for recovery and support.

Works Cited

https://www.imf.org/en/Publications/fandd/issues/2021/09/climate-change-and-inequality-guivarch-mejean-tacon et#:~:text=People%20with%20the%20lowest%20incomes,clean%20water%20and%20affordable%20food
https://www.weather.gov/crp/hurricane_harvey

Untitled

by Monica Becerra

I always wondered how a raging ocean could leave the body dry, how the blazing sun could still allow one to be frozen in fear, or how a child's blistered feet could continue walking through the pain. The ocean I know leaves your body drenched with water dripping from your head to your toes, but my father says the ocean he knows was one in which he was stranded and only a drop of seawater on his lips was able to try to hydrate him as he crossed the sea out of Cuba. The sun I know leaves one at feverish temperatures with sweat covering their bodies, however my grandmother says the sun she knows wasn't hot enough to stop her sweltering body from freezing in fear as she made her way out of the murderous wilderness of Mexico. The feet I know stop and rest anytime I feel even the smallest uncomfortable pebble in my shoe, however my mother knows the bloody feet of her childhood as she continued making her way to the land of the free and the home of the brave.

They made it here to the climate of Texas, where hurricanes run rampant and the sun heats the earth. A family who proved they belonged here, overcoming the challenges that prove them as brave and free, yet they are not seen that way. I have seen men who call themselves audacious, yet prey on the vulnerable lamb. I have heard women who shout that they are unbound, yet they have never known captivity. I have seen children bully those who are different, while they are unaware of the beautiful diversities of the world. How can they pretend to have sight, yet be so blind when they ridicule those that they refuse to truly see.

The hurricanes that pass through this town flood the streets where injustice runs rampant. But this is not the only hurricane that occurs. There exists another, one inside the minds of my family. One hurricane that simply torments them as they flood their memories with pain. As the water reaches their porch, so do the floods of the past, reaching their ankles as it tries to drown them out.

But there exists a cure. A cure to the venom of the floods. The temporary eye of the storm is something that can become a stable reality. Faith. There exists a fire within their eyes as the waves rise to their knees. Somehow an unwavering faith in the future, knowing that perhaps one day it will be better. This faith exists even when they know they will not live to see this change, but hopefully their children may, hopefully their children will live with only one hurricane in their lives. The hurricane may pass one day, but there will always exist one, tormenting the minds of immigrants until the day they find their cure.

Looking above in the city in a plane, it all looks so small. Similarly, the unwavering faith blazing in one's eyes can appear to the hateful eye. However, to me and many others, this fiery blaze consumes the body, lighting their path and guiding their steps as they traverse the cold wet planes of this earth. The hateful eye watches them and spews out words of filth, words that do not encourage or motivate, but rather words that destroy homes and nations. With the fire, one cannot be put out. With the fire, one is stronger than who they previously were. With the fire, one cannot be put down by the hate of those void of it. They cannot and oftentimes will not comprehend the power of the flame, for they are afraid of how strong the flame can be in the face of such adversity.

Although the journey here is a trail of bitter blood, sweat, and tears, it is never in vain if one has the flame. The words spoken as a prayer keep the holder of the flame bright. They know that all they do and all they might is for a purpose, for the future. For when they look ahead and witness the earth, they know that despite the hate that arrives in a hurricane, they maintained their flame. And so I sit still in our dining room. I turn my head to the right. There, my grandmother is preparing lunch to feed her family. I turn to my left. Looking out the window I see both my parents repairing the damages done to our home. The hurricane is now gone, but I know in a year I will hear reports again during the season. However, I do not fret, for I know that only one hurricane will flood our lives, the other now just a distant memory of the past, one that we have overcome.

Decimation
by Jenna Bleakley

Listen to the howling,
The screaming of the pain of the wind.
The agony it must feel.
Whipping, whirling, destroying anything in its path.
Trying to find something solid to stabilize itself.
Wishing to make others feel the pain it does.
Listen to the water,
Rushing to fill any empty space with panic and fear.
Where will the people go to escape this despair?
Fear gleaming off the people's eyes,
Panic coursing through their bones like the water.
Where will they go? What will they do?
What about their family, friends, and neighbors?
The thunder so furious.
Destroying everything it touches.
The houses rattle.
The houses whistle.
Fear and terror shock through the people.
Homes lost, animals lost, history lost.
These are the effects of extreme weather.

Extreme Weather and Inequality
by Brenya Boudreaux

Extreme weather events and inequality are closely intertwined. The impacts of climate change are felt most acutely by vulnerable communities, exacerbating existing inequalities in access to resources, economic stability, and social support. It is essential that efforts to address climate change and extreme weather events prioritize the needs of marginalized communities and work to address systemic inequalities. This can include initiatives such as investing in renewable energy, supporting low-income communities in adapting to the impacts of climate change, and prioritizing the needs of vulnerable communities in disaster response and recovery efforts. By addressing the intersection of extreme weather events and inequality, we can work towards a more just and sustainable future for all.

Untitled
by Brianna Brottem

The day before, everything was fine,
The day of, rain and lighting filled the sky
The long night to come was shown by a "stay safe" message.
Nobody knew the terror you would bring.
Four long days you sat on your throne within the clouds.
You cried and cried until you could weep no more.
Your sadness and heartache destroyed everything I loved.
Those unaffected laughed as if this was an extended weekend.
The memories, the possessions, and my past life were swept away.
Hours were spent salvaging, digging, and hoping for a reminisce of
      a memory.
Days were spent volunteering for people who lost clothes, food, and
      medicine.
The year after, your tears no longer remain here,
but the hurt and pain you caused linger at every storm.

Untitled

by Hannah Campbell

Living in Texas at 17, I have experienced extreme heatwaves, hurricanes and winter storms. Texas is known for hot hot summers and unpredictable weather. Living in Texas we experience a wide range of climate challenges.

Where I live we are susceptible to hurricanes, and especially areas along the coast are the forefront of these weather events.

I've seen communities struggle to be able to just evacuate and have to come back and face the aftermath of hurricanes hitting. The recovery can take years and years.

Heatwaves in Texas can be so hard on the elderly especially for the low-income families. I feel like they suffer the most during this time. Having access to air conditioning and clean water can be hard to come by for them.

I remember a couple years ago we experienced a really bad winter storm. So many were left without power. Grocery stores running out of essentials, gas stations running out of gas. Communities faced really bad hardships.

I feel like Texas, like many parts of the world too, struggles with inequalities that make the impact of extreme weather events even more devastating.

Low-income families are often unable to prepare well enough, and evacuate when needed or recover from disasters.

The consequences of extreme weather impacts our health and well-being. Heat-related illnesses, air pollution, and a lack of healthcare resources. These have long-lasting effects.

For kids education is important and extreme weather can disrupt it. Schools were destroyed and closed down, leading to canceled classes and missed opportunities for learning. Also, the lack of a stable house can disrupt their education, social development, setting back their future.

As a 17 year old Texan, I believe in the power of youth voices to drive change. Schools should teach about the consequences of climate change. In school I've learned the importance of climate action and the impact of extreme weather events. I've learned of the importance of renewable energy and stricter environmental regulations that prioritize climate. I believe that education is the key to addressing extreme weather and inequality. We should continue to learn and to raise awareness about the impact on communities and schools and continue to be part of the solution.

Extreme Weather and Inequality:
Bridging the Gap for a Resilient Future
by Lola Carr

Extreme weather events, such as hurricanes, floods, and heatwaves, have become increasingly frequent and severe in recent years. While these events pose a threat to all communities, regardless of socioeconomic status, it is often the marginalized and vulnerable populations who bear the brunt of their impact. This essay aims to explore the relationship between extreme weather and inequality, shedding light on the disproportionate effects on disadvantaged communities. I will explore some of the notable events in recent years and provide personal testimonials. In addition, by examining recent statistics and scholarly research, I will present the evidence with the aim of providing a deeper understanding of this pressing issue and highlight the urgency in bridging the gap to ensure a more resilient future.

Extreme Weather Trends

The effects of climate change have resulted in an alarming increase in extreme weather events worldwide. According to the Intergovernmental Panel on Climate Change (IPPC), global warming caused by human activities has significantly contributed to the rise in extreme weather occurrences (IPCC, 2022). These events, including hurricanes, floods, and extreme heatwaves, have devasting consequences on both ecosystems and human communities.

In recent years, record-breaking weather events have dominated news headlines. One such event was the record-breaking Atlantic hurricane season in 2020. According to the National Oceanic and Atmospheric Administration (NOAA), this season saw a total number of 30 named storms, surpassing the previous record of 28 in 2005, the year I was born. The impact of these hurricanes was devasting, causing loss of life, destruction of homes and infrastructure, and displacement of communities along the Gulf Coast, East Coast, and Caribbean Islands. The economic toll was also immense, with estimated damages exceeding $40 billion. To make it personal, in 2017 Tropical Storm Harvey hit my town of Beaumont, Texas. Harvey, initially a Category 4 Hurricane, dumped nearly 60 inches of rain in my city, Beaumont, Texas. This resulted in catastrophic flooding in Beaumont and the Houston area. According to news reports, Harvey caused at least 68 direct fatalities and an estimated $125 billion in damages, making it one of the costliest natural disasters in the U.S. history. It also exposed the vulnerability of low-income communities and highlighted the disparities in preparedness and response efforts. Many marginalized communities, particularly those living in flood-prone areas, faced significant challenges in evacuating and assessing essential resources during and after the storm. For example, due to lack of resources and failure to evacuate, families were being rescued from their roofs, were displaced, and separated as they went into shelters across the state to escape the storm. The unimaginable fear and terror this storm caused as it pounded through dumping flood waters was unforgettable. Two years later, in 2019, Tropical Storm Imelda came through my town and caused another catastrophic flood that many people won't see in a lifetime. My middle school was impacted by this catastrophic event.

Another impactful storm along the Gulf Coast was Hurricane Laura. Although Laura did not directly affect my town of Beaumont, it did make landfall to neighboring towns in Southwestern Louisiana and around Southeast Texas. Laura brought destructive winds, heavy rainfall, and a dangerous storm surge in 2020 as a Category 4 hurricane. This catastrophic event resulted in multiple fatalities and extensive damage to homes, infrastructure, and agriculture. The impacts of Hurricane Laura were particularly devastating to Lake Charles, Louisiana. For example, in Lake Charles, Louisiana the storm left behind a trail of destruction with buildings reduced to rubble, widespread power outages lasting for weeks, and disrupted water and sewage systems. The storm's impacts were compounded by the lack of recovery from a prior storm less than a year before and the ongoing Covid-19 pandemic, which strained local resources and made recovery efforts even more challenging. A friend of the family, whom I will call John for the sake of this essay, shared his distressing account of the aftermath of Hurricane Laura with my parents and me. He spoke of the devastation to his crops and infrastructure, which left him and his family struggling to recover both financially and emotionally. John emphasized the need for greater investment in climate-resilient farming practices and infrastructure to protect against future extreme weather events. As can be seen through personal testimonials, these storms caused extensive damage and displaced thousands of families. Similarly, unprecedented heatwaves have swept across various regions, leading to increased mortality rates, particularly among vulnerable populations, such as the elderly and low-income communities.

Now, that I have highlighted just a few of the extreme weather trends, I want to present to you some evidence on its impact on impoverished communities. While weather itself does not discriminate, its effects are disproportionately felt by marginalized communities exacerbating existing inequalities. Socioeconomic factors such as income, education, and access to resources play a significant role in determining vulnerability and resilience to extreme weather events.

Furthermore, low-income communities often face higher exposure and limited adaptive capacity to extreme weather due to several interrelated factors. First, these neighborhoods tend to be in areas vulnerable to flooding. Insurance premiums are generally higher in flood zone areas. In return, many low-income families cannot afford to properly insure their homes. In addition, limited financial resources make it difficult for residents to invest in resilient infrastructure or relocate to safer areas during times of evacuations from storms. As a result, they are more susceptible to property damage that they can't repair, displacement from families due to shelter availability, and the loss of livelihoods.

Additionally, disadvantaged communities may lack essential resources and support that can aid in recovery from damage and displacement. Although there are government assistance programs, such as FEMA, it is often not enough help during a major crisis that causes major damage. A study conducted in 2021 found that low-income individuals face greater difficulties in accessing post-disaster assistance and recovery programs, leading to prolonged periods of distress and limited opportunities for rebuilding their lives. This disparity further widens the gap between the affluent and the less privileged, perpetuating systemic inequalities.

Addressing the Gap: Policy and Community Initiatives

To address the issue, a comprehensive approach that combines policy measures and community-based initiatives is essential. Governments must prioritize climate change mitigation and adaptation strategies and ensure an equitable distribution of resources and support. For example, more tax dollars can be invested in climate resilient infrastructure to protect vulnerable communities. This includes improved flood control mechanisms, such as better drainage in the cities, earlier warning systems that are equal throughout the at-risk areas, and enhanced building codes to withstand the higher-grade storms. It is also equally important to consider the specific needs of disadvantaged communities during the planning and implementation process to avoid exacerbating existing inequalities. Moreover, policy interventions should aim to reduce social and economic disparities that leave marginalized populations more vulnerable to extreme weather impacts. This involves addressing affordable housing, accessing adequate healthcare, and getting a proper education, as these factors contribute significantly to community resilience.

Community-led initiatives also play a vital role in bridging the gap between extreme weather conditions and inequality. Grassroots organizations within our local community can partner together to empower families through education and skill-building programs that develop resiliency and adaptive capacity. For example, organizations like Some Other Place and The Salvation Army can engage with marginalized communities within our community and involve them in decision-making processes that can foster a sense of ownership and ensure that their unique needs are considered in the planning process. Proactivity is the key to creating an effective bridge.

In conclusion, extreme weather events pose a significant threat to all communities. However, it is noteworthy that my region of the Gulf Coast alone has experienced its share of record-breaking weather events in recent years. From hurricanes, to floods, to extreme heatwaves, these events serve as a wake-up call to the urgent need of planning. Events such as these have had profound impacts on human communities and communities of low socioeconomic status, causing widespread devastation, displacement, and exposing existing social and economic inequalities and disparities. Real-life examples and testimonials from those affected emphasize the urgent need to address climate change, build resilience, and ensure equitable resources to protect vulnerable populations. This direct correlation between extreme weather and inequality demands urgent attention from policymakers, communities, and individuals alike. By bridging the gap through targeted policies, equitable resource allocation, and community engagement, we can create a more resilient future where the impacts of extreme weather are equitable. It is crucial that we act now to ensure a just and sustainable world for future generations to come. Let's bridge the gap!

Life Turned Upside Down
by Victoria Ceja

"Life is like a storm. Storms bring in the gloomy clouds, lightening, and even the natural disasters, but at the end it's also a time for growth and rebirth which is life," is a quote said by someone anonymously. In real-time events, the storm of life was created by Hurricane Harvey back on August 25, 2017. This catastrophic event led many businesses and houses to become destroyed, the rebirth of new businesses, and to my life changing. The hurricane changed my life in multiple ways because, for the first time, I felt the adrenaline of being in a situation that would be televised on the news and worried about what to do with my pets, but it also made me grateful for what I have.

It was raining horribly on a late Tuesday night. My father was relaxing in the garage peacefully hearing every raindrop that fell to the ground while my little sister, my mom, and I were inside pacing back in forth in the house wondering if we had to do an emergency evacuation. "Everything's fine. You don't need to worry, it's just a bit of rain," were the exact words my father had said to us. We all trusted what he said and found something to distract ourselves with inside the house. I laid on my bed scrolling through my phone without a care in the world since I had always trusted my dad's words. As confident as my father was about us not having to do an emergency evacuation, he was just as confident to realize that the water was beginning to rise. He alarmed the rest of the family, but continued by saying there was nothing to be afraid of and that the water will eventually go down. Ironically, the water was already about 5 to 6 inches in the house about 10 minutes later. For the safety of the whole family, we decided it would be best to evacuate. Grabbing all of our belongings, but deciding what we actually needed instead of wanted wasn't as easy as it seems. I, as a 6th grader at the time, was going through a surge of adrenaline that led me to fail at focusing on what tasks I was doing. In a blink of an eye, I was seated in my eldest brother's warm car.

However, I had 13 birds at that time. I refused to leave them behind and let them suffer by themselves, so we did the most logical thing which was to bring them with us. It was too late to evacuate out of the city, so we resorted to staying at my grandparent's house for the time being. The only difficult thing about this was that there were 2 other families staying at my grandparent's house which meant there was no room for anyone, not even for my birds. Thankfully, my brother was able to make room in his house for us, so we were able to give everyone else more privacy and less packed which made my grandmother relieve some stress that was on her shoulders. As we drove to my brother's house, I looked out the window the entire car ride just taking in the tragedy left behind by Harvey.

As I looked out the window that faced the street, the view was heartbreaking. Every building I turned to look at had been destroyed by water. Cars that were incapable of moving any further were abandoned by their drivers. Helicopters were flying left and right trying their best to save the people who were in need of being saved. Families, even with newly born children, were on the roofs frantically waving their arms seeking safety. People who were homeless and had built their makeshift homes sat in agony in front of where the closest thing they could call a home was once built. The sight horribly saddened me. Even looking back at this traumatic event, I learned to be thankful that we had left in time and to know that we were all safe. Although we made it out safely, we were one of the several families who had to reconstruct their house which took almost a year to complete and safely move back into.

In conclusion, the disaster of Hurricane Harvey took a toll on many Americans during 2017. Thanks to Hurricane Harvey, I was able to be thankful for everything that I have, but also made me feel an extreme amount of adrenaline and sadness for the loss of others.

My Little Dog
by Ashley Collins

my little dog had a coat shaded like deep, dark sand
his hair glistened like a mirror, reflecting all light.
we keep him neat and tidy
but when he went out to play
he never stays that way.

he loved the adventures of the neighborhood
but hated it when it rained
hiding as the thunder clapped and the wind roared
my little dog, "don't be afraid," i'd say
the rain will soon wash away

one day, a mighty storm came through with no sign in the air
my little dog wanted to play, but "only for a little while," I'd say.
as the clock ticked, there was a rush, then thunder rolled.
where is my little dog?
i yelled for his name, but i was clouded by fog and rain

a hurricane.
water swelled the streets, surrounding nearby houses
where was my little dog? where did he go?
filled with fear and heartache,
i waited, but my little dog never came back.

along he laid, somewhere under
my heart was left with a hole.
just as black as his coat
concaved with sadness, my soul would just be left to float

Nature's Temper
by Eve Winters Compton

Extreme weather, nature's wild display,
In the sky's theater, it has its say.
The sun's scorching blaze, relentless heat,
Or blizzards that blanket in ice and sleet.

Tornadoes dance with a furious grace,
Twisting and turning in a fearsome chase.
Thunderstorms rumble, lightning's bright streak,

A breathtaking spectacle, powerful and unique.

Hurricanes swirl with a mighty spin,
Unleashing chaos, a tempest within.
Droughts parch the earth, leaving it dry,

While floods rush forth, with waters high.

Extreme weather tests our resilience and might,
Yet it reminds us of nature's untamed flight.
In its grand spectacle, we find both awe and fear,

Respecting the forces that are always near.

Nature's Fury
by Guadalupe Contreras Bernabe

There is extreme weather all around the world, some worse than others. Hurricane Harvey is an example of extreme weather here in Nederland which was a devastating tragedy that left many people without homes or in a worse situation than they were in before, my family also being a victim of this. My family experienced being unfairly judged and criticized, refusal to help us throughout, and no help afterwards.

In the area where I lived, it was obvious that it was going to flood pretty quickly and badly because of the lake right behind our house and the ditch nearby. Therefore, most people in our neighborhood were evacuating as soon as they heard the confirmation and warnings about the hurricane coming. My mom and dad were trying to evacuate too, there were eight of us, not including our dog. My youngest brothers were only one and four years old and the youngest was already sick. My parents were stressed and desperate to evacuate before it was too late but we had nowhere to go. Back then we were very financially unstable and our cars were already struggling to work so we could not afford to leave the city or state to stay somewhere else at that moment. Even so, my parents had people criticizing them for not leaving and putting their kids in danger which only made the situation and their stress worse.

It didn't take long for it to flood our area because of the ditch and lake I mentioned before. The water was rising fast, so by then it was too late to evacuate by ourselves, and there was nothing left to do but wait for the help we heard was coming. We waited for a while before we finally started seeing boats going around our neighborhood to check how many people were in need. When they came to us they asked how many people we had in the house and my dad told them we had eight, plus our dog. My dad told them about my youngest brother and how he was only one and already sick enough, hoping they'd be quick with getting us out of there. Hearing this, the men said they'd come back to help us to safety as soon as possible. However, we didn't receive any help for a long time. We saw boats passing and helping everyone else around us, and when my dad would wave his arms to get anyone's attention, they would come over and tell us they were checking how many people they needed to help in the neighborhood, despite the fact that we had seen them taking people in their boats already. My dad was furious and kept trying to get help because it seemed to be like we were the only ones not getting any help. Even an explanation would have been better than just leaving us there to think that we were being ignored. Finally, a boat came to us and told us that we were too big of a family to help and that we'd take up too much space and probably more than one boat, which they didn't want to do because they wanted as many boats available to help others. My dad understood that much so he asked if it was possible if they at least took my mom and my younger brothers somewhere warm and safe, but they refused for some reason. We didn't understand why that wasn't possible and it was never explained to us either. We just had to deal with being the last people to be evacuated, which we were very grateful for but had just hoped it had come sooner for my little brother, whose condition ended up worsening.

The aftermath was probably the worst part of it all. Since we were already struggling financially, the damage the hurricane had done to our house and vehicles did not help our situation whatsoever. Our house was a disaster, the outside of the walls were torn, the pipes were damaged and not working, our yard was a mess, and our family car was now completely not working and busted because of what looked like a hit it had taken. My mom applied for help when she heard we could do so but our help was denied because there were more serious cases out there and we still had a roof over our heads so we could consider ourselves lucky. I understand that there were more serious cases out there but we did not have the financial stability to repair the damage that the hurricane caused alone. We went a long time with the pipes not working and the car not working, which belonged to my mom who bought our groceries while my dad was at work. We were not able to get any groceries for a while because of this. The rest of the damage, like the yard and the house walls, my dad managed to fix himself with his own tool with the help of nobody else but my mother and my siblings and I occasionally.

My experience does not begin to cover what other families went through and the inequalities they experienced, but it shows the inequality we had to deal with that left us struggling even after it was already all over. The damage these extreme weathers cause can't be reversed, but help can be provided to fix that damage for those in need of it.

Extreme Weather and Inequality:
A Closer Look at the Connection
by Angela Cooley

In today's changing climate and extreme weather occurrences, causing unprecedented dangers exacerbate existing social injustices and economic imbalances. It is vital to explore the link between extreme weather conditions and inequality since these aspects comply with each other but also leave long-lasting impacts on communities and individuals.

Extreme weather incidents, like hurricanes, floods, and heat waves, tend to disproportionately impact marginalized communities. This unequal effect is due to multiple factors, including limited resources, inadequate preparedness, and insufficient infrastructure. The damage caused by such events intensifies the pre-existing inequalities within particular communities.

For example, low-income areas often lack the necessary resources and infrastructure to counteract the consequences of extreme weather conditions. This includes access to emergency preparedness plans, healthcare facilities, and resilient housing. Consequently, people living in these regions are more vulnerable to short-term effects during such events and more prone to long-term health issues that worsen over time.

Moreover, disadvantaged groups usually have little political power or representation in determining policies related to climate change and disaster mitigation efforts. As a result, these communities are less likely to obtain the required funding or assistance for projects that could reduce the negative impact of extreme weather incidents on vulnerable populations.

Another aspect contributing to inequality is the relocation or displacement of individuals after an extreme weather event. Factors like insufficient finances or limited housing alternatives push these communities deeper into poverty cycles. Forced out of their homes due to inhospitable conditions, many have no choice but to rebuild their lives in new locations where job opportunities are limited or nonexistent.

Therefore, it is not enough just to recognize the influence of extreme weather on inequality; it is also crucial for policymakers and stakeholder groups to devise tactics addressing this interrelatedness. Effective climate adaptation initiatives should emphasize inclusive community involvement while prioritizing need-based resource allocation.

Safeguarding against future severe events necessitates a forward-looking and comprehensive approach to cultivating resilience through social, economic, and environmental strategies. Plans and policies must emphasize fair resource distribution, enhanced representation for marginalized groups, and a dedication to addressing the systemic injustices impeding progress on these issues.

Untitled

by Brady Corcoran

The rain pummeled and the lightning roared. It had been days since the rain ceased. Hurricane Harvey was among us. As I watched the news cast and saw how bad the hurricane had gotten, I wondered how bad others were being affected. As I saw more and more videos across social media of people getting rescued by boat I wondered how I could help as well. My house was fortunately on high ground and we only got water about three fourths of the way up our driveway. It was scary and almost reached our house but still our home was undamaged by Harvey's madness. When the rain let up and my street became low enough to drive on I knew we had to do something to help our town and others affected.

As the rain started to let up my phone lit up from a text from my youth pastor. It read, "Those that are willing and safe enough to come, the church is being opened up as a refuge center for the people that escaped their flooding homes." I immediately told my mom that we needed to help the people out and help our youth pastor take care of these people. So we jumped in the car and slowly made our way through the flooded streets to our church. When we arrived there were about five people already there wet, scared, and in need of assistance. My mom and I jumped in helping these people out by assisting them with food, water, and aid. Once we were done assisting those people, it was at that time more and more people began to come in. One by one, victim by victim they came to escape the hurricane. My mom and I with the help of a couple other of my friends and their family members continued to help and tend to the victims of the vicious hurricane.

The church gym and youth center began to be full and the building began to become crowded. We eventually had to slow down how many people we could take in. More people needed to be helped and not enough people could reach other families to leave the church. We thought of many ways and other solutions so we could house all these people so we didn't have to stop taking people. Unfortunately, we had done all we could do for the people of our town. We eventually had to stop taking people in because of how crowded the youth building and gym got. Disappointed that we couldn't find a solution, we just focused on what we could control. And what we could control was helping all the people we had in our care. Throughout the night we cared for those people as the rain continued. Then once the rain started to sputter out and people were able to get ahold of their family members, one by one the gym started to clear of refugees.

Our work was done, the people got the help they needed and we were able to give a dry roof to over 500 people. I don't know why our house didn't get flooded and so many others did flood. I didn't ever really understand why such a hurricane could be so wrathful to an area. I thought of how unfair it was that we had to experience this. But then again I have to remind myself, people all over the world go through things that are hard and unfair. People go through hardship and people will face trials, it's how we face them and conquer them together as a community that matters the most.

How Did I Get Here?
by Marshalei' Daniels

As I sit here staring off into space, listening to the lyrics of Deborah Cox's "How Did You Get Here, a song playing on the radio, I chuckle and ponder over how I ended up in my current situation. At the tender age of 17, I never thought that I would become homeless, but life can be unpredictable. So, what made me homeless? Let me share my story with you.

It all began before I was born. My parents got married in July 2005, and shortly after, a hurricane (Rita to be exact) hit our area. I've been told that I was a hurricane baby, as I was conceived in the aftermath, and born nine months later. As I look at pictures from those days, I recall the story of my homecoming. My mother was hesitant to bring me home because the men were scheduled to work during the week of my due date on the roof, and she didn't want the noise to disturb my first few days home. That's why I lived with my grandmother for the first 6 months of my life until the roof and ceiling were repaired.

The home where I spent my childhood took a lot of beating from all the extreme weather over the years—Rita (2005), Humberto (2007), Ike (2008), and Harvey (2017). We once had aluminum siding on the house, which began to fall off due to the weather. My father took that as a hint and removed the rest, exposing our home to the elements. When we arrived home, my mom was furious, and many arguments ensued over the conditions of the house. So, my dad did his best to insulate the house. As he would often say when I would ask what he was doing. "I'm keeping the air from going out in the summer and wind from coming in through the cracks in the winter. He would wrap our house in whatever material he could find. I knew my house was ugly and would be embarrassed to have friends over. One time, my teacher brought me home after school, and one of her kids said, "Mom, look, it's the monster house!" to which she replied, "Boy, hush your mouth!" I was crushed. But looking back, I was happy because my family and I were together.

I miss those days. I miss being in my own home, my own room. Don't get me wrong; I'm grateful that my uncle allows me to stay with him and his family, as it has truly been a blessing. Both of my parents worked hard, and every time they sought assistance, they were told they did not qualify. "You make too much money, your credit score is not high enough, you should have had home-owners insurance, and our agency can't help you." Growing up, I didn't know much about the haves and the have-nots. I just knew we didn't have a lot. We just had each other, and that was enough for me.

After years of trying, my parents were finally able to secure a loan to repair the house. I finally had a home that I could be proud of. My mother was no longer starting arguments, and I was elated to have friends over. However, that was short-lived because right before the pandemic hit, we were told we had three days to vacate. Unbeknownst to my mom, our house was sold for taxes. Man, I never want to see my mama cry like that again. Packing up my room and saying goodbye to all my friends was one of the hardest things I've had to do. Today, we no longer have our home, and my family is split. My dad had to retire due to his medical depression. I don't understand this adult stuff, and I hesitate to jump into this arena. I would often overhear conversations that would leave me puzzled about the working-class poor. Those who work and get no assistance versus those who don't work yet have access to every resource. There is a bible verse 2 Thessalonians 3:10 that says "For even when we were with you, this we commanded you, that if any would not work, neither should he eat." My parents did everything right yet help came too late. As it stands today, the only way my mother could qualify for any assistance is if she quit her job, had more babies, or decreased her income. The middle class is what holds everyone together, but there is no one to help them, hold them, or have their back. I hope shortly, the middle class will be considered more in the distribution of resources. We all know that extreme weather is no respecter of class, status, or socioeconomic background. So, it's up to us to level the field and help keep families together.

Life After Ike
by Tacota Deiss

Rebuild, sometimes easier said than done. How do you rebuild a home built by the worn-out leathered hands of a passed relative? Connected to a house containing many generations of blood, sweat, tears, love, and many memories, decades on that property nestled in the same little town. Have you ever been through a life-changing natural disaster, where your deep family roots have been ripped up and scattered like spider webs in the wind? Natural disasters come in many forms of distributive actions and within a matter of seconds can change the whole town's lives. Hurricane Ike, the unforgiving disaster of 2008, was a Category 2 hurricane that brought a twenty-foot wall of salty sea water that surrounded our little island and submerged most of the surrounding peninsula. Like many disasters, normally unpredictable with no way humans can stop these awful acts of nature, all anyone can do is wait out the storms to start picking up the pieces left behind. The devastation in our tiny community was heartbreaking, and the obstacles of rebuilding had a large influence on how individuals would recoup, rebuild, and go on with their lives.

Of course, I was just three years old when this storm blew in, so I had to go interview those older than me who witnessed and lived through it for them self and investigate the areas affected. I discovered some interesting information about High Island, the little town where I grew up, which is standing entirely on top of a salt dome about thirty feet above the Bolivar Peninsula. Let me just say that if you haven't met someone who is several decades older than you, I recommend you pull up a chair, enjoy a cup of coffee, be quiet, and simply listen to all the tales you didn't realize you needed to hear. Like for instance, did you know Jean Laffite? Nope, well that's ok, because neither did I until a simple conversation turned into a four-hour history lesson. Buried six foot deep, in our small town lies Charles Cronea, who was one of Laffite's cabin boys. Apparently along with Cronea, a family member of mine decided to leave the ship of Jean Laffite and set up residence in that small town. Unfortunately, there is not recorded documentation of my family member that joined Cronea, but according to the oldest man I know on the island and a few family members and friends, this story is part of my history. High Island before Ike, consisting of over six hundred people, contains one of the most sought-after bird sanctuaries for migrating birds, marshes full of gators, and of course the beach. High Island is nothing fancy and you won't find any celebrities playing volleyball on the beach but what you will find is family homes and a small school that consists of approximately two hundred and fifty kids ranging from Kindergartens to Seniors. These are the good ole folks, who will wave at you in passing, sit on their front porches drinking coffee, they will give you the shirts off their back and always offer a lending hand. Extending down from the hill of High Island is the Bolivar Peninsula, about thirty miles parallel lying between the gulf coast and canal. From High Island to Port Bolivar is a peaceful place that is home to so many wonderful people, great family run restaurants, places you can go fishing, take horseback rides on the beach, listen to the waves roar from your windows, and so much more.

Ike was no surprise

Ike would be reaching land that September 13, the people of the Bolivar Peninsula were aware of the storm approaching, and proceeded to take precautions as they have done in the past with any storm rolling in. It is not uncommon to not find many evacuating, around here people hunker down to ride out the storms. Hunkering down consists of covering windows with boards, pulling all loose items inside, and stocking up on enough supplies to last a week or even two. Past storms brought destruction to the roofs and maybe a few blown out windows, but no one was prepared for the life damaging effects that Ike was bringing to town. When I say hunker down, no I don't mean they go to basements or storm cellars, that is not a luxury here, instead they are hunkered down inside the closets, bathtubs or hallways in homes that are on stilts standing fifteen or more feet off the ground, where normal rainstorms cause the houses to sway in the wind. To say the least, these people are brave and not going to let a hurricane with over a hundred mile an hour winds make them a coward running them out of town. As the night fell on the Bolivar Peninsula fast, the overly confident storm riders finished checking their flashlight and batteries, fueling up their generators, filling up their cars with gas and charging their phones. Nestled in all they could do now was wait for the storm to roll in and move quickly out of their lives.

My mother's anxious voice sent chills down my spine as she spoke about Ike. Little did I know that storm transpired a pivotal point in our lives as well. While the storm loomed over the gulf, my mother and brother finished off the last storm preparations and loaded the car up ready for the early morning departure. Trying to be overly prepared to avoid and prevent reliving the nightmare once endured from the previous storm, Hurricane Harvey, pregnant, stuck in her car over ten hours on the highway, trying to get to family, where she felt hopeless running out of gas, food, and water. Needless to say, my mom is not the hunkering down kind of person, she is super afraid of even the small everyday rainstorms. It only took the flickering of the lights and elevated winds, for my mom to change plans to load us up and head north before the clock even struck midnight. Fortunately for us, my mother is not a procrastinator and took action quickly, otherwise, we would have been stuck on High Island surrounded by water with no way out the next morning. Even though my mom had managed to get us to safety, she was still worried about all those who stayed behind to ride out the storm.

Hours before daybreak Hurricane Ike made landfall, emerging powerful winds along with an extensive storm surge immediately bulldozed the Bolivar Peninsula, the silent horror grabbed hold of everyone. Dump trucks were deployed to the beach to begin rescuing those who were trapped and helpless inside their homes and vehicles attempting to flee the rising water. As the water unexpected rapidly increased, people resorted to chainsaws to cut through their roof tops in order to escape the rising water while they waited for helicopters to rescue them, and cows and horses were running to the small hill to take whatever shelter they could. The peninsula's situation had undoubtedly gotten worse, survival mode was being implemented in a variety of ways as homes were torn from the pillars and vehicles completely submerged under water. Two men floated away to another town thirty miles north of the peninsula, having to avoid not only debris but gators, deadly snakes, ants, wild boars, and other dangers. Another man refused rescue staying behind to care for his beloved tigers that could not be transported by helicopter. Regretfully, a member of our family passed after being abandoned for an extended period of time while attempting to flee her home from the floodwaters, by the time the water subsided enough to get the dump truck to her it was already too late. I witnessed an abundance of tears stream down the cheeks of friends and family as they stammered through the heartaches and disappointments reliving their harrowing stories from their hellish catastrophe.

Once Ike had departed and rescues crews completed their duties, the scattered debris that lingered behind floated in the high standing waters, bringing further grief, suffering and lifelong disturbance to the Bolivar Peninsula. The National Guard was called in to continue the efforts of rescuing on top of securing safety. All those who evacuated were eager to return home but those who had stayed home were being forced to leave. At this point there was no running water, no electricity, no way to get in except by boat, those who could get in were lucky as many were turned away. The first to return from my family was my grandmother, who snuck in saying she was going in to get all our families medicines and animals, making a promise to leave, but once she made her way in, she refused to leave. When she went to check on our house the roof had collapsed and cows filled our yard. The residents of High Island lost a lot of roofs, and those who stayed behind had already started going around applying some sort of tarp to any one's homes that was in need. Remember I told you that this town was a help one help all kind of place. You didn't have to beg for help, or worry if you would be left alone to pick up the pieces because at any giving point you would have a yard full of people there ready to pitch in. It was about a week after the storm that people were allowed back into the town, which included my family. When my mom decided to take us back home to start cleaning up and helping our town, she life would be tough knowing that food and water would be scarce and taking baths would be far apart. We spent almost six weeks living in a town that had no electricity, no running water, eating MRE meals or from a food truck that served us lunch. My mom said she although it was one of the hardest times of her life she had never felt safer than living in that moment, in that town, learning the value of family and friends.

Now, I had to tell you a little bit about the background of this storm and the impacts it bestowed on to our little community before getting into the inequalities of the Bolivar Peninsula. Most of the people rely on jobs that were damaged, underwater, or just washed away, and without means of making money there was little hope for those people to purchase items, foods, clothing, and things that had been lost in the storm or they needed to survive. Most of the people I interviewed felt they were left alone struggling for help from the Government, and the reason they felt was due to the poverty and lack of diversity. No celebrities had rushed to start a fund or bring supplies in, and why was that they all wondered, why didn't they get the attention of the world when they needed the help. These people didn't want handouts, they wanted nails, tarps, port a potty, fuel for generators so they could keep working and rebuilding. So many people on the peninsula had felt betrayed by their government, as they watched and had previously watched how assertive they were to other towns. Not only did they feel deceived by the government, but those who had insurance also began to face other problems, like not being able to get aid once the government started helping and the insurance companies refusing to accept their claims. The last thing these folks needed was more suffering while trying to find the help they required, given that more than half of the neighborhood had been washed away.

After investigating the effects of Hurricane Ike with my family and friends, I discovered that until a person physically goes through traumatic events that have an immense influence on life, the heart does not fully know how to feel, and the eyes can never see as those individuals do. It truly puts into perspective how quickly life can change, embracing their suffering, their tears, and their voices trying to speak of all that was lost. Items taken for granted such as baby pictures, door frames lined with marks marking growth, or family heirlooms that held great meaning for them that will never be replaced. Although I was only three, Hurricane Ike altered the course of my life. Who would I be today had Ike not ripped apart my mom's life.

Survivor
by Raul A. Diaz

All I saw was rain falling down,
The trees swaying in the heavy wind
And our shelter destroyed, left to drown.
Will I ever get to sleep with a roof over my head again?
Will I ever get to eat a good meal again?

I always knew my family had less wealth,
And that never bothered me, until the storm hit.
Like a debt collector it came without warning,
And with it came the realization
That wealth comes to those lucky few
Whose only limit was their imagination
And their families' bloated wallets.

The help from the community was grand,
Helped us stay in an emergency shelter.
But this was just a temporary measure,
As after that neither me or my family knew
Where we would go, or where we would live.
Everyday I wonder if I'll make it to the next,
My life feels like it's as fragile as an insect.

As I was born into this, so were my parents,
And so we're their parents.
We were immigrants who immigrated
To escape our home country's crumbling economy.
Compared to us, everyone else seems so free,
Full of choices that they can make without worry
That they won't have enough money,
Or enough rights.

Then I realized, there were more,
More people like us, who struggle to live everyday.
No matter the time, no matter the place,
Someone is always struggling.
Millions across the globe, suffering,
Only ones who'll never starve are those at the top,
They always laugh in their mansions making champagne pop.

But I know that eventually, we'll win,
That we'll take our disadvantages
And throw them out into the trash.
We'll solve our problems and surpass
Our limitations. Even if it takes a century or ten,
Eventually, I'll win, for them, for us.

Changes
by Jasmine Do

"We cannot prevent hurricanes or earthquakes, floods or volcanic eruptions. But we can ensure that both people and communities are better prepared and more resilient." —Miroslav Lajcak. August 25, 2017 was a day to remember. Hurricane Harvey had struck the southeastern part of Texas destroying homes, businesses, and most importantly lives. It was a life changing event for many people, especially for me, an 11 year old at the time. For the first time, I experienced the most devastating event to occur in my life, and it felt like I was drowning inside the hurricane. That year I learned to be grateful for everything that I still had after the hurricane.

On a day thought to be like any other, a Category 4 hurricane named Harvey struck the small city of Port Arthur. I was outside bringing in groceries my family had bought in a hurry because supplies were being sold out everywhere around my city. My family was in a state of panic like no other, and at the time it didn't occur to me what I was witnessing. The wind had picked up and it was sprinkling outside. I thought nothing of it because I knew it was hurricane season, but little did I know that there was a hurricane on its way to my home. I remember very clearly my mom had the TV on in the living room, and I heard the news telling us to evacuate and go somewhere else. My mom thought it wasn't that serious because she knew that hurricanes never come toward Port Arthur, so we ended up staying at home that day. All the phones in our house had gone off with weather alerts and the sirens of multiple emergency vehicles blared outside my house. I was worried about my dogs outside hoping they would be okay since I knew we couldn't take them inside. In a state of panic my family told me to get my dogs into our backyard storage room where they would be safer and sheltered from the storm. Later into the day Harvey hit Port Arthur, my sisters were charging their battery packs and stocking up on flashlights to use if the lights went out. A branch from a tree in my backyard came crashing down onto the roof of my house scratching multiple windows on its way down. The screeching noise was a sound I'll never forget. I came out of my room and discovered the fallen branch and told my parents, but they couldn't go out into the blazing rain. Our power went out a little afterwards and the struggle to stay cool hit us. We sat in my dark living room, wishing the power would turn on, trying to cover up any leaks in my house, and hoping that the backyard didn't flood. When the storm had subsided the streets were flooded. Many of my neighbors came together with their boats trying to get as many people as they could. I was fortunate enough to have a house built on a hill, so the flood didn't affect me as much.

I was becoming grateful for everything that I still had after the storm. Looking around that day, I realized that many people have lost their homes and their stuff alongside it. One of my best friend's houses was destroyed and even years after Harvey they couldn't recover from the amount of money they had to loan to be able to rebuild their houses and basically their lives. Although they applied to multiple organizations to help with the rebuilding and shelters nobody would help them. They had to rely on what they already had and live somewhere else for the time being. I felt so grateful that I didn't lose that much compared to everyone else, but it was unfair for the people who didn't get the help they needed. The several cars abandoned on the streets, the businesses that had their roofs ripped off from the top of their heads, everything had changed and all I could do was sit around and hope that it would get better. The local news station was outside my home reporting everything that was happening. It was unfair that the people who didn't have enough money had to be outside in tents in the aftermath of the storm. People who once had the comfort of living in their homes had to be outside struggling to find food due to the storm. People should be able to get the support they need no matter how rich or how poor they are. We are supposed to help one another get through tough times but during those few days after the storm, it was a game of everyone for themselves.

It shows that there should be changes made throughout the system on extreme weather support organizations. They shouldn't be based on whether a person is rich or poor, they should be able to help everyone. I am grateful for being able to have the luxury of still being able to live in my home, but I am devastated by the fact that people couldn't recover from Hurricane Harvey.

Navigating the Storm
by Kayde Dotson

I guess you could say I am a hurricane baby. In 2005 when Hurricane Rita hit, I was in my mom's belly. Mom, dad and my older brother all evacuated to Texarkana, Arkansas. I've only been told these stories, because, you know, I was *in utero*. While in Texarkana, my brother broke out with chicken pox. After the storm passed my hometown, Beaumont, Texas, the family traveled home.

In 2008, Hurricane Ike showed its evil head in my hometown. Once again, I was only 2 years old when we evacuated this time, still being told these stories by my parents and grandparents. Beaumont was flooded with 8–10 feet of water. Our home was completely destroyed! Our family had to stay in a hotel for weeks and weeks. My mom tells me that her search for diapers for me was horrific because the entire town was flooded with no stores to buy diapers. My dad told her it was a good time to potty train me!!!! Needless to say, I was potty trained in 2 weeks. The rainbow at the end of Ike I guess you could say.

Moving right along with life, Hurricane Harvey hit in 2017—I was 11 years old at this time. I vividly remember this one. Over 60 inches of rain flooded my city once again. Houses on my street in my neighborhood were unrecognizable. Some houses were completely under water, only seeing the roofs. My house was flooded with 4 feet of water in it. We lost everything AGAIN!!!!! Both of my parents are teachers, so we were blessed to have a steady income in order to survive.

Lastly, Tropical Storm Imelda showed her presence in 2019. Our home didn't flood this time, but most of the schools did. We were out of school for weeks while the schools were repaired. People in other parts of the country panic when they hear of a hurricane in the gulf, as for me, it's just another day of living in Southeast Texas.

25,360 Years[1]
by Kowen Ducote

Criminal negligence
Is a crime
That incarcerates the individual
For 2 years.

To acknowledge the inequality
Pervasive throughout the United States,
It would be dishonest to speak of these problems
Without mentioning the injustice embedded within our government.

If a congressional leader,
Signs off on a bill
That kills thousands
He is not penalized.

If he wages a war,
Funds an ongoing conflict,
Legislates violent occupation of foreign nations,
Or terrorizes impoverished neighborhoods,
He is not detained.

If he destabilizes developing countries with differing philosophies,
If he develops a violent smear campaign,
Justifies acts of terrorism,
As a "war on terror,"
He is not convicted of a crime.

If he destroys our Earth,
Shuts down attempts to revitalize our soil,
To revitalize our people,
He will not be held accountable.

For the rule of law does not apply
To a "representative democracy"
And mother nature's retribution

---

[1]   "25,360 Years" is the prison sentence that would be inflicted upon an individual who was convicted of the damage caused by the 2023 Hawaii Wildfires, only accounting for criminal negligence and arson. We do not hold our governing bodies to the same standard of those who consent to be governed.

Will not be felt
By those in power.

In Hawaii earlier this year,
A devastating wildfire occurred
That injured ~160 people
Devastated ~2,500 buildings,
And brought ~100 people to death.

Amongst this tragedy,
A somber, brave niece spoke out
Out of respect for the passing of her beloved uncle, Jantoc.
"My uncle was known for playing music across the world
And the island of Maui for 30-plus years."
". . . [a] happy-go-lucky guy [whose] smile stood out.'
He was always smiling."
"(I'll miss) his calls for the silly stuff.
Buying things for him, ordering online because he didn't know how to work it.
Or you know, fighting with his iPhone because I had bought him a new one
He didn't know how to work with."

It's hard to compartmentalize the depths of sorrow
Inflicted upon the people of Hawaii due to this tragedy.
Their losses will forever be incomprehensible
To an emotionally-detached,
Criminally negligent,
Barbaric regime,
That is purely concerned with profit.

Works Cited

Eaton-Robb, Pat, et al. "A Family, a Beloved Sister, 2 Senior Housing Residents. These Are Some of the Lives Lost in Maui." *AP News*, AP News, 18 Aug. 2023, apnews.com/article/hawaii-wildfire-victims-maui-lahaina-67cbaaed21545c1af0f6ee7c582322e3.

Hamilton, Kevin. "Hawaii's Climate Future: Dry Regions Get Drier with Global Warming, Increasing Fire Risk." *The Conversation*, 16 Sept. 2023, theconversation.com/hawaiis-climate-future-dry-regions-get-drier-with-global-warming-increasing-fire-risk-211379.

Weather and Inequality
by Emma Ferguson

Being Southeast Texas high school students most all of us have been affected by or know someone who was affected by extreme weather events caused by climate change, in the form of a hurricane. We have seen firsthand how the impact of a major natural disaster can drastically change a community. Houses and businesses are destroyed leaving thcsc individuals affcctcd without homes or jobs. Food and resources become scarce and everyday living conditions are altered from what we are used to. For most in our area we are able to recover and life returns to the way it was before the event, but the impact is felt harder and longer lasting for individuals in lower socioeconomic and marginalized communities. These individuals often face challenges to access food and water, have forced displacement, impacts to their livelihood, and health issues. Climate change related weather events are a global issue and certainly not limited to our area, but almost always impact people living in poverty the most.

Climate change in general refers to the long term shifts in weather patterns and temperatures. While some people argue that these changes are natural, humans have been the main source of climate change since the 1800s, primarily by the burning of fossil fuels. According to the recent data from Oxfam's research with Stockholm Environment Institute the wealthiest one percent of humanity are responsible for twice as many emissions as the poorest fifty percent. However the impact these emissions cause to our global climate and environment will affect low income areas the most. Climate change intensifies the separation between individuals with access to resources and the individuals who do not. This is something we see time and time again when a weather disaster occurs. Underprivileged areas often wait months or years for assistance from underfunded relief efforts to rebuild, while their wealthier counterparts leave the area all together or use their resources to rebuild. This is a pattern that will only become more common according to many experts.

Inequality in climate change is not limited to wealth inequality, but is also seen in gender inequality. Women in poverty are at the greatest risk of being affected by the impact of global climate change. According to the UN women and girls account for eighty percent of people displaced by climate change. Seventy percent of the 1.3 billion people living in poverty are women. Women in impoverished areas have limited access to and control of goods and services. Most of these women do not have any decision making power in their communities and therefore do not have a voice in change or action. According to Global Citizen, "These factors, and many more, mean that as climate change intensifies, women will struggle the most. In fact, the Paris Climate Agreement includes specific provisions to ensure women receive support to cope with the hazards of climate change." Climate change also increases violence against women and girls. Displaced women and girls are at a higher risk of violence, including sexual violence according to the UN High Commissioner for Human Rights. There is also an increased risk of human trafficking and forced marriages. Access to an education becomes increasingly hard for women and girls affected by climate change and make them dependent on their partner. This increases their risk of economic, physical and psychological violence.

Climate change affects us all as a global community. We have seen the impacts in our own communities, but we were fortunate enough to also see a major rebuilding of our area. A majority of the homes and businesses affected by these extreme weather events in recent years were able to be repaired or rebuilt. We need to understand and educate ourselves that this is not necessarily the norm. We happen to live in a socioeconomic community that had the resources to rebuild without much disruption to our food, water, health services, and education. There is a vast majority of our global community though that are not as fortunate. The only way to see change is to educate ourselves about the inequality in climate change and for us each to do our part to make a difference.

Untitled

by Emily Flores

The day where the waters flooded the once safe haven that I was told would always shelter me at the worst times had flipped my world upside down as I truly understood the meaning to be in 'someone else's shoes.' Five years ago in 2017, Hurricane Harvey struck Jefferson County and left death, destruction, and despair behind its path that would leave scars for years to come. Watching Harvey consume my county while observing the aftermath unfold before my eyes, I could truly see the perspective of those who are at a disadvantage and were treated with the inequality of socioeconomic status.

The thought of knowing there is some sort of hierarchy with money even though some people tend to push these thoughts in the back of their minds, relish in these barriers between people, or even ignore this concept altogether. I'm no saint of this hierarchy as I even choose to give it the cold-shoulder. I've seen the towering homes in rich neighborhoods and the poor who live near grocery stores with their makeshift homes. However, as humans we turn a blind eye to this socioeconomic hierarchy and usually only gather or socialize with those of the same level of status rather, we realize this or not. The upper-class get the best connections as their money can afford the treatment and are usually first in line with connections or have more resources available to them. The middle-class being in the in-between usually has the biggest spectrum as some are well off and have access to resources or just living comfortably with some sources. Then the lower class who must use creative thinking skills to get the job done when obstacles occur. As a middle-class citizen myself, facing these obstacles I've had my range of opportunities whether my family had the capability to gain aid as the upper-class or having to get imaginative like the lower-class.

Even though Southeast Texas has a hurricane season, I haven't seen a natural disaster that was catastrophic as long as I lived and have gotten to experience it firsthand until Harvey. As a middle school student at the time hearing that a hurricane was coming towards Jefferson County, I was ecstatic because I would have some days off from school because to me, Harvey was another small inconvenience that would cause black outs and meager floods that I could float in with a floaty. I stood corrected because Harvey was way further than my expectations as water raised higher and higher until cars on my friend's elevated driveway were starting to go underwater. This was nothing I had experienced before as my family, family friends, and I were carrying valuables and furniture up the stairs in case the water rose up high enough to flood the inside of the house. Placing the weighted sandbags in front of the doors observing the strong winds blow trees away and the heavy rain pouring down with lightning striking everywhere lighting up the sky made me understand the servility of the situation at hand. Yet, instead of worrying about the people who have no strong shelter to protect themselves are facing this hurricane head on even though they are already at a disadvantage my mind was elsewhere, but as a kid I had no idea how the world worked.

After the hurricane had dissipated and the sky started to clear the aftermath was still laid as water levels were still significantly high with houses and cars destroyed and dismantled with the county in ruins. The constant news update regarding Harvey at the time displayed the casualties from all over Texas, but that's not what shocked me the most. Seeing my own county in ruins is what impacted me the most, people's homes annihilated with nowhere to go and churches opening to provide shelter. At the time everyone seemed to be hand in hand like a community supporting each other. However, as time passed and reconstruction and building started, while the schools picked back up everything was good it seemed. Yet, certain situations piqued my interest like how I overheard kids who still didn't have housing and now have barely any clothes to wear and unfortunately didn't have the money to afford clothes at the moment. The majority of the houses that were being worked on or had finished were houses that were located in the suburbs or private neighborhoods. The media had slowly started to decline in the telling of the aftermath after higher status homes were recovering along with schools and jobs were back in business. There were no updates about lower-class homeowners or homeless people. The churches also resumed service meaning that the people who were being sheltered had to leave at some point. People who were at a steady or were at an advantage before Harvey resumed life while those who were in the lower socioeconomic status were still facing the outcome of the hurricane with little aid now. Even after a year I still pay attention to houses and people and even then, I heard these same people facing complications due to Harvey even though majority of news outlets concluded that most of the communities were bouncing back yet they were forgetting about some of their citizens.

Harvey made me realize that socioeconomic status has a huge role in natural disasters and how the disadvantage is put at an even more disadvantage when tragedy strikes and there needs to be more help within our communities to make sure that everyone can come back together.

Rising Waters, Deep Divides: Unraveling the Systemic Issues of Weather Inequality
by Horacio Garcia

It was 4 a.m. on a long morning of a storm's landfall, one that was supposed to be "just another storm." This thought flooded the minds of the vast majority of inhabitants of Southeast Texas, who have previously endured and overcome the hardships that storms bring along. However, something was different on that very night. 4:15, 4:30, 4:45, and there was no sound of the pumps that were meant to save the city from deluge. It was not until 5 that morning that the very structures supposed to protect us made any sign of life. Regardless, it was simply too late to stop the ordeal that was taking place throughout Jefferson County.

As rain fell for what seemed like ages, even Port Arthur's "well-maintained" drainage system could not stop the streets from turning into rivers. Naturally, the water had nowhere to go and began to pile up until it reached the inside of homes, businesses, and essential services, all of which are someone's livelihood. For many, this was far worse than any home invasion that could have possibly occurred, as it took more than just personal belongings. Hurricane Harvey meant the end of the road for many Port Arthur families, who either did not have the means of recovery or did not want to risk another serious disaster.

This storm was ruthless, and continues to be what we as Southeast Texans think of when recalling natural disasters. It impacted the rich and the poor, the old and the new, and the young and the old. When people think of weather inequality, they think of the disaster itself as being unequal. The reality is that we cannot control Mother Nature, but we can control how we prepare and respond to what she has to bring.

Throughout the Golden Triangle, many neighborhoods encountered the same fate: swamped with water containing who knows what? However, drastic disparities came after the storm passed during the recovery phase, despite facing the same wrath of a storm. While many residents in wealthier neighborhoods in Mid County were able to quickly flee their homes, those on the older, south end of the county were not as fortunate. Because the Texas National Guard remained overwhelmed by the extent of the storm, civilians from both inside and outside the county came together and organized an extraordinary rescue effort that I, along with many others, will forever be thankful for.

Once the water finally receded, the recovery process was the same, until it wasn't. Wealthier, predominantly white neighborhoods filled with those who had the means to fix their homes recovered quickly, while less fortunate ones suffered significantly. In fact, for many of those neighborhoods, it took nearly three years to see visible progress take shape. The sad truth is that this was not the first time that such unequal recoveries took place.

Back in 2005, New Orleans suffered a worse yet similar fate in which the vast majority of the city found itself underwater. While homes in the city's predominantly African American east end had water up to their roofs with people desperately trying to escape, more affluent areas of the city were more concerned about looting than the human toll of Hurricane Katrina. That being said, the areas that remained dry brought back a dark past in the city's history in which the city's affluent and largely white residents built their homes closer to the Mississippi River, which was the highest ground in a city described as a "cereal bowl."

Here in Southeast Texas, the same can be said about many homes here. Up until 2018 I lived in Griffing Park, a once predominantly white neighborhood in Port Arthur known for its large oak trees and quiet environment that was one of the few areas in the city left largely dry. Although the neighborhood nowadays has many more residents of color, the legacy of inequity remains.

To truly overcome weather inequality we must recognize that they do not result exclusively from natural disasters, but can also be deeply rooted in historical and systemic struggles. These disparities are interconnected with the much larger issues of poverty, racial injustice, and environmental degradation. In order to address the topic we seek to discuss we must first solve these interconnected problems.

Looking forward, it's important to take inspiration from the resilience of communities in Southeast Texas and others around the world who have come face to face with the harshest force of the elements. Their stories highlight the power of solidarity and our capacity to come together in times of need. We should embrace this more than we already do to bring about lasting change.

Furthermore, let's not forget that government agencies have the responsibility to equally address crises, and not fall into failure and embarrassment as we have seen time and time again. It's a shame that we must trust volunteers and neighbors more than the government who is constitutionally obligated to "protect the people." It took days to get a federal and state response during Katrina, and months or even years for the less fortunate to return to their neighborhoods. That was 18 years ago, but it seems like we have advanced nowhere. Therefore, I call upon government entities to pledge for disaster rescue and relief policies that do not exclude large swaths of the population. Moreover, before we send billions of dollars overseas we must first fix the aging and neglected infrastructure that is responsible for much of the monetary damage associated with natural disasters.

As we embark on the journey towards weather equality in a quickly changing world, let us remember that it is not only about facing the storms but also addressing the systemic disparities that shape the extent of their impact. We stood strong during Harvey, Imelda, and countless other events that tried to shake us to our core. However, in order to continue doing so, we must acknowledge the lessons we have been taught.

Extreme Weather & Inequality
by Kimora Garrett

Extreme weather has affected everyone whether they know it or not. Severe weather is not only classified as a natural disaster, it can be any form of excessive heat or cold for an extended time. I am originally from Las Vegas, Nevada, the desert. I have been no stranger to the extreme heat because I grew up in it. Now that I have moved to Texas, the climate is different, something you have to adapt to. The weather in the two places is not the same but not completely different but it still affects everyone around.

The weather in Nevada cannot be completely compared to that of Texas because of the location and the climate differences. This can cause great inequality between that of the citizens of the state. For instance, the homeless population average is higher in Nevada than in Texas, with a rate of 24.20% compared to 8.30%, as stated by the World Population Review in August of 2023. More people in Nevada are homeless during this time but they might be going through a different experience weather-wise. Seeing as Texas has a more moist heat while Nevada has a scorching heat, why would it be?

The severity of homelessness is epochal everywhere. These are the people who can't protect themselves properly against the strong and intense weather. Many of them need help but won't be able to receive it because they are homeless. The homeless are seen as dirty and poor rather than struggling and in need of help. They are stereotyped and it is unfair to them as humans.

Homeless people probably go through unspeakable things daily and the effects of the extreme weather conditions don't make it any easier. The National Center for Biotechnology Information stated,

> The most frequent causes of death were circulatory system diseases (33.80%) . . . whereas a small number was caused by infectious diseases, while a relatively large proportion of deaths were due to tuberculosis (2.15%). Most deaths oc curred in the conditions of cold stress (of different inten sity). Deaths caused by hypothermia were thirteen-fold more frequently recorded among the homeless than for the general population.

This further explains the extent weather conditions, hot or in this case cold temperatures, have on a person's body and how detrimental it is to receive the help you need before it's too late.

I have had a few encounters with severe heat. I can recall this specific memory from my childhood, so to speak, when It was so hot outside that I practically passed out in the car due to the heat. It was the summer of 2014 or 2015. I was in the car with my sister and cousins. The car had no air conditioning and ended up running out of gas on the side of the road. At this time, I was eight or nine years old, so as kids we weren't a great help in this situation. We had to sit still because it was so hot, movement only made it hotter. While we were waiting for my cousin's husband to come with the gas, it got to the point where I was drenched in sweat. I don't remember going to sleep or getting tired, I just remember being loopy and out of it. By the time I regained consciousness, I realized the car was moving again; I was getting out to get hydrated. My story demonstrates extreme weather and how it can affect the average everyday life. Not only do you remember it but it becomes a part of your learned experiences.

Within The Eye of The Storm
by Alyssa Garsea

On August 24, 2017, the day our lives changed forever. The first of many hurricane warnings of category 5 hurricane Harvey was sent out sending the town buzzing instantaneously like an angry hive with locals filled with anticipation and fear as they dreaded the worst that the beast Hurricane Harvey held. Due to the unprecedented situation, most schools in Texas were left with no other option but to close their doors, leaving the majority of students at home. Unfortunately, despite all the preparations made, the catastrophe that was about to occur in the South could not be prevented.

Within a few short hours, the small worries soon turned into reality. As I woke up to the sound of an eerie beeping I grew curious as to what the pestering sound was. Walking out of my room I was hit with a harsh reality. I watch and listen in awe as the weather channel reports a category 5 hurricane named Harvey was headed directly towards my hometown, Nederland, TX. My heart that was once in my chest jumped to my throat as the anxiety filled my 11-year-old body. Summoning every ounce of courage within me, I forced myself to shake off the fear and continue with my day. The hours that followed seemed to stretch endlessly, each minute feeling like an eternity on that particular Friday. No matter where you went you couldn't escape the rain. The sound of heavy raindrops gradually disappeared from my attention as the hours went by. Slowly, streets began to be swallowed by the rain poured onto the ground.

As the day turned to night, the streets and lawns began to disappear. How have we gotten this much rain? When is it going to stop? Many parts of the town were already experiencing flooding. Homes, nursing homes, and businesses were taking in water. We made sure our family was safe and then settled in for the long night ahead. We stayed up in our family room watching the news, watching report after report of how Harvey was initially planned to be a small storm but very quickly became a horrible situation for our community. The last I looked out of my window, all I could see was that we were on an island. Every home in our neighborhood was on an island of their own. The rain had not stopped for over 24 hours now. We watched patiently praying that the water would stop creeping up on our home. As the minutes, then the hours passed and the rain continued, we saw the water was near our home. Before we knew it, water was intruding into our space, our home.

We were not the only ones. We were lucky compared to others. Our home had damage but after some cleaning and rain-soaked flooring, furniture, moldings, etc. we were able to live at home.

We made it through the stressful 36 rain-filled hours! We woke up to a sun-filled sky! It was hot too. Many parts of the community had water recessed. So many were dealing with the emotions of their losses. Homes were destroyed. As you drove around town, everything was muggy, everything seemed damp. There were neighborhoods filled with flooring, carpet, furniture, you name it on their lawns for garbage pick up. It looks like a warzone. Even after the rain receded, we realized we were on an island for some time. Bridges around our community had water near this from the rivers or some bridges washed out. Every little community had to be independent. It was tough for a bit.

But I have to say that although this experience was hard, I saw something very beautiful. I saw our little town come together. Friends and family help each other to clean out their homes. Strangers and communities also go home to home to help tear out wet carpets and move furniture. Individuals and groups cooked meals for those who were working non-stop or had no means to get a warm meal. The towns were a mess but they were beautiful at the same moment.

As with a hurricane, there is beauty and calmness within the eye of the storm. I saw firsthand how although we experienced the storm, there was such beauty and calmness within the eye of our storm in our small town. I saw that we can weather what Mother Nature may send our way. I say this, Mother Nature has sent us many hurricanes during my life; I think we have this experience done. And this summer's heatwave we weather that storm as well. If Mother Nature wants to send us a snowstorm at Christmas this year, we will take it with gratitude and enjoy some hot chocolate.

Natural Disasters
by Gabriella Haley

Mother Nature dictates our city
Tornadoes, floods, and heavy downpours all within her capacity.
Infuriating lightning strikes down a tree that's been in my family for years
Howling wind rips my roof off from above me and sees my tears.
Agitated floods drowns my furniture right before my eyes

Mold, disease, and sickness creeps into my family's facility.
Calling for help is my only ability.
Spewing out my worries and fears
They disregarded them with sneers.
How could they leave us here to die?

Was it our lack of wealth and pity?
Denied help only left me feeling gritty.
Why does our economic status determine who hears?
The answer is clear—
We need more allies.

Community outreach will enhance our city.
Access to clean water, food, and shelter is all in our communities' capacity.
Stepping up and helping others will benefit us for years.
Seeing change brings up tears
Everyone should have their basic needs to live in my eyes.

My Love, Mostly Hate Relationship with Hurricanes
by Olivia Harms

How much would you hate being named after a hurricane that destroyed your childhood home. If the answer is a lot, then I agree with you. My mother was about to name me Katrina but changed it last minute, due to the massive hurricane that devastated Louisiana. After this storm, it was the catalyst to move to South East Texas. Although I love where I live and couldn't imagine growing up anywhere else, everywhere has its downside. In this area it is the unpredictable weather, in particular hurricanes. I have seen first hand the devastation that has come from these storms. Yet, each storm has only brought our communities closer together, as we rebuild stronger and higher quality. My family's business , a compilation of hard work and dedication, is a testament to this. These events allowed me to identify how weather damages shaped my family's real estate business, my personal growth, and our community's resilience.

The wrath of weather, particularly hurricanes, brings a multitude of problems. These problems sway from massive wind damage to roofs, garage doors, and all areas of the house to busted pipes and flooding. There is also the risk of falling trees on houses, cars, and people etc. As the weatherman announces an incoming storm, we brace for property damage, power outages, displacement of families, and the emotional toll of uncertainty. As this is stressful for all, for my family this issue is multiplied by thirty. Weather issues ripple through our business, causing stress and uncertainty. As many of the houses are in different areas there is no way to relax when there is a hurricane in the midst. The concern for the occupants of the houses is number one, making sure them and their families are safe. To do this my dad, with the help of my brother, goes to each house to put boards on the windows and place sandbags where they are needed. I see this issue in my parents' face as they start getting calls from leaseholders wondering what is going to happen and how they are going to prepare.

Living through these challenges, I've witnessed firsthand the truffles and the stress. This is particularly stressful for them because of the financial strain on their business. Thankfully they have flood insurance on all of their houses, but this does not take away from the issue of unknown costs. The financial issues skew from paying employees, leaseholders unable to pay rent, and houses being destroyed or damaged heavily. After hurricane harvey, I saw my parents really struggle financially and emotionally dealing with the stress. I was finally old enough to see the true effect these issues have on not just my family but others in my community as well. I felt the overwhelming stress as me and my mother strapped down items outside and lugged outdoor furniture inside. I have this specific memory of feeling extremely scared as me and my family packed our bags to evacuate. My sister walked into my room and took one look at me, she stopped and gave me a hug and said, "it's going to be okay, we are all here for each other." I remember feeling an immense amount of relief as we set out to an unknown location. We return back to our community and homes heart-wrenched. Seeing my mother's and father's properties damaged was very tough. Yet, in the face of adversity, we've found resilience and solutions. As we went through this trying time I saw the major effects this had on our community and family. I was recruited to help rebuild and patch up the damage from the hurricanes. Me and my cousins made the best out of the situation, as we worked tirelessly to help my parents. At my church, we set up to help as many people as we could. Seeing all of my friends and family come together to help strangers who needed it, in light of their own problems, brought me an insurmountable amount of joy. Realizing the passion and love that my community was willing to give to each other taught me a very important lesson. This lesson taught me that in all trying times, there is always a positive.

In conclusion, weather issues pose significant challenges, but they also teach us resilience. These traumatic times allowed me to inspect how weather issues affected my family's business, my personal growth, and my community's resilience. Hurricanes will always be an issue in the area that I live in. My family's business and my fellow community members will struggle in these times but in the end there is always a positive. I choose to examine the good in these situations and look at the negative as a reason to grow and bring the communities together.

The Hurricane That Changed Lives
by Colby Harrington

August 25th, 2017, a day that millions of Texans will never forget. A storm that brought about an eternal rainstorm that ended with utter destruction and lives devastated. Hurricane Harvey, a name so infamous it is now retired, made its landfall, and it would change my life as well as the millions of other people who were affected by this devastating storm.

During that time I was only 11 years old. I vividly remember seeing all of the news coverage of an approaching hurricane, and I thought to myself "Well it shouldn't be too bad." My grandparents had downplayed the severity of the storm and said it wasn't going to be too bad, and so we stayed home when the hurricane hit. The skies became gray and ominous, and soon the pepper colored clouds rolled over us, and the rain began. It did not sprinkle, instead the rain poured down onto the earth with no warning as if it were trying to attack us. It began during the afternoon, and as the day went on the rain never stopped. The constant sound of the ferocious rain slamming onto our roof is a sound I'll never forget. We watched in horror as the flood water began to creep up higher and higher towards our house. We hoped that the water wouldn't enter our house, but it did. I'll never forget hearing the sounds of my Nana and sister crying as the water started to slowing flood into our home. I tried to stay as calm as possible as my grandparents told me and my 8 year sister to pack up whatever we could so that we could leave the house. I had to reassure my sister that everything was going to be ok, and that we were going to be ok. The water was cold and the sky now completely dark. The roads weren't visible, so you wouldn't know if you were turning onto another road or straight into a ditch. We didn't know where to go, so we first tried hotels. When we couldn't find any hotels we decided to park the jeep underneath a covering at the local mall. That's where we slept for the night. We finally came back home the next day, and we took a look at all the damages. A foot of water had flooded our home, heavily damaging it and a lot of our belongings. The Remodeling Era soon took off as we had to tear down our walls, and remove everything out of the house. We, just like everyone else affected by Hurricane Harvey, had piles of dry wall and furniture that was destroyed by the storm in our front yard. Our house had to completely be remodeled because of the sheer amount of rain the storm had brought upon us. We were lucky and fortunate to be able to have our house back, unlike many unfortunate people.

For a lot of people, Hurricane Harvey was the end of their homes or businesses. The storm caused 125 billion dollars worth of damage, and disrupted businesses for weeks and even months. It was the second costliest natural disaster only behind the devastating Hurricane Katrina. Thousands of people were displaced due to their homes being destroyed, and some never were able to get their homes back. My great grandma had a beautiful house that my entire family would gather in for holidays or big family get togethers, and then Hurricane Harvey leveled it into the ground, never being rebuilt again. Many, many, many more people went through the same thing or something similar to that as their homes were destroyed by the relentless storm.

Hurricane Harvey was a unique natural disaster in which it lingered over Texas and caused a devastating amount of flooding. Some areas in Texas received more than 50 inches of rain within a 4 day period. A storm to that liking is unique to Harvey. A hurricane that will be remembered in the hearts of Texans as a storm that destroyed their homes.

Another Way
by Sakara Harris

There has to be another way
Here comes the flood . . . Another city's washed
away
No parks here are safe to play
Another school's gone another overdraft on the
way
There has to be another way
It's so hot the children can't go out to play but
this is Poverty-ville nothing you can say
The water's polluted nothing to drink today
There has to be another way
There's so much I can say but nothing I can do
Even those upstate have so much they've gone
through
Starting with tornados and then the earth
beneath starts to shake I believe that's called an
earthquake
And everything has a cause but they're not
looking for them the Black Robes up top just
create
new laws
And then raise the amount of money spent so
the poor can't even afford to pay their rent
There has to be another way
The gangs in the streets don't make this struggle
no better
They're so worried about who's getting clout or
moving more "paypa"
Or if they see a "opp" they gotta pull up
Another young mind influenced by yet another
viral screw-up
There has to be another way
They've even made laws to legislate the way we
choose to procreate
Killing our kin we can not win
It's time to find a solution to the condition we've
been put in
There has to be another way
I don't wanna march when all they'll do is send
another platoon

Taking our young brothers and sisters way too
soon
Another mother mourning the lost of a child
And all of the fake love she'll receive is wild
Why do we care so much about carrying guns
When people choose to use a park or school as a
shooting range for fun
it's strange
There has to be another way
No time to be on the internet trying to find the
next trend
When my fist goes up all knees will bend and
heads are bowed
Not much marriage cause not many can honor a
vow
There has to be another way
Is there a way to finally stop this pain
To finally stop pointing fingers and really look
into who's to blame
No reason to have others hanging their head in
shame
When we are all just pawns in someone else's
game
There has to be another way

      Be better than those
who've came before us for we are
greater than our predecessors—

(author's notes)
* Opp - (Opp)osition or someone you have conflict with
Pronunciation: (aw-p)
* Paypa - money or cash
Pronunciation: (Pay-Puh)

2023 Climate Crisis
by Syndi Hatchel

In the days now, there are many upon many crisis' that we are having, the biggest one being our climate and inequality. Some people don't truly understand what's going on with our world and population nowadays. Everyone thinks it's all fine and dandy but the reality is much more brutal than it may seem.

Our world, the Earth we live and walk on every day is slowly crumbling and becoming nothing anymore. Our older generations want all of us younger generations to fix this all, all of these pollution, fires, and other disasters that are occuring, when really we all need to work to better the Earth and to help the weather. The days are getting hotter which is leading to droughts, which then leads to fires. Homes of animals are being destroyed daily because we can't get together to fix our climate that is in deep need of help. Our own homes are at risk because of the fact that fires start, fires spread and get to our homes, the places we have grown up and made memories in. There is so much at risk because some people think it's okay to throw litter into our water, onto our grounds. We as a group need to work to get our planet back on track, back to the way it would want to be. So many things are being killed, destroyed, buried under rubble of our land because there is so much that we aren't doing, things that could be easily done. Throwing trash away in the proper way, using only resources we need, watching the things we do such as driving our cars, could bring us a long way. Such simple things, things that we have been accustomed to doing, are destroying our atmosphere and making our weather and climate much, much worse than we could have ever imagined. It shouldn't matter who you are, what you believe, what skin color, or sexuality, we are all responsible for what our Earth has become and what it is going to come to.

People like to overlook a lot of things, but people also tend to look too deeply into things that shouldn't matter. Race, just the color of our skin, something we can't even control, is something that people take into so much consideration to determine how exactly they treat each other. White people will look at a person of color and immediately feel uncomfortable just because of what they see. No one gets to know each other anymore before they just feel obligated to accuse or stereotype people into a group based on their skin. It's the same thing for people with different sexualities, people will look at them differently just because of the fact that they love someone different than normal. A man can love a woman openly, but the moment it becomes a man loving a man, a woman loving a woman, then it's a problem. Even if it's a man loving a trans woman, or a woman loving a trans man, there's no winning for people who love differently but all as equally. Religion can be a big reason as to that type of thing, why others hate on each other so much. People shouldn't let their religious belief control how they react to something, including people of other religions. Catholics and Baptists go head to head, thinking both are going to hell just because of their beliefs, even though both are a subgenre of Christianity. Christians think of Pagans as devil worshipers which isn't true, but that's the stereotype for them that other people from other religions have made. Even if you decide to not believe in anything or believe in multiple gods, people always end up having a problem with it. In religion, and even outside of it, gender has a huge role in how other people treat each other. Women get stereotyped for not being strong, powerful or sometimes even smart, they're expected to know how to clean and cook well and are degraded when they can't. Men get stereotyped for having to be masculine, tall, strong, they're expected to like cars, working out, sports and aren't expected to cry, and are also degraded when they don't like the things the world has forced to be a norm. Then people who aren't either or, or who like to flexate between being masculine, feminine or androgynous, are all then called names, all because they are being true to themselves. It's not fair to anyone that's different to another person, whether that be for their race, gender, sexuality, or religion. In every group there's inequality, no matter what subject, where it is, or who it's about, there's more than likely going to be some type of stereotype and inequality in the mixture.

Extreme Weather & Inequality
by Deacon Hebert

Extreme weather events like hurricanes, floods, droughts, and wild-fires have become increasingly frequent and even more severe in recent years, primarily because of climate change. Although one can argue the cause of climate change, one cannot argue its effect on extreme weather. Another thing people cannot argue about is the unequal impact of extreme weather on different populations world-wide. Inequality, in terms of vulnerability and resilience, plays a massive role in the consequences of extreme weather. This paper explores the relationship between inequality and extreme weather and its broader implications for society.

Extreme weather events hit vulnerable populations the hardest, whether these vulnerabilities are economic, social, or demographic. Lower-income communities and areas are more likely to flood due to lack of access to disaster-resistant infrastructure, and they can face issues evacuating during emergencies. Also, marginalized groups can face discrimination and unequal access to resources, compounding their vulnerability to extreme weather. Additionally, as extreme weather events become more frequent and severe, some communities may become uninhabitable. This forces people to migrate, leading to climate-induced displacement. Vulnerable populations often face barriers when seeking refuge, as well as discrimination and prejudice when arriving in new areas. In this way, inequality becomes a driver of social tension.

On the same wavelength, economic disparity needs to be addressed; extreme weather can exacerbate this disparity. The cost of recovery from these events is immense, and people with limited financial resources may struggle to rebuild their lives. In contrast, wealthier individuals often fare better due to insurance for their homes, meaning they can recover quicker. Also, environmental injustice can be applied, for polluting industries tend to be located near low-income communities, so these communities face the dual threat of climate change along with the limited resources to adapt. This issue remains relevant beyond national borders. Developing countries, which have contributed far less to greenhouse gas emissions, often lack the resources and technology to adapt to extreme weather events, making them especially vulnerable to a changing climate.

Inequality and extreme weather are intertwined challenges that pose serious threats to global well-being. As these dangerous weather events increase in frequency, the disparities in vulnerability, resilience, and recovery will become more pronounced. Addressing these inequalities requires a comprehensive approach, including measures to build resilience in vulnerable communities, reduce emissions, and promote equitable access to resources and opportunities. Only through collective action can we hope to mitigate the devastating effects of extreme weather events and create a more equitable and sustainable future for all.

Untitled
by Scott Lucian Helt

Extreme weather is when the weather goes totally crazy, like when it rains so much that rivers overflow and flood towns, or when super-strong winds from a hurricane blow everything away. These crazy weather events are happening more often, and they're not fair. Some people get hit way harder than others, and that's not right.

Imagine you're living in a place where your house might get flooded every time it rains a lot. Now, imagine you don't have much money to fix things up or move to a safer place. That's what's happening to a lot of folks who don't have much money. They're stuck in places where floods or other extreme weather can mess up their homes, and they can't do much about it.

It's not just about homes, though. Some people have good jobs and can afford to fix things up when a storm wrecks their stuff. But others don't have good jobs or any savings, so when disaster strikes, they're in big trouble. It's like they get hit twice—first by the weather, and then by the cost of fixing things.

And when these extreme weather things happen, people can get sick or hurt, too. If you don't have much money, you might not have good access to doctors or medicine. So when a storm or heatwave hits, it can make your health problems even worse.

Now, imagine your town has old, broken-down pipes that can't handle all the rain from a big storm. When those pipes burst, it's like a water explosion, and it messes up everything. Rich neighborhoods can usually afford to fix these pipes quickly, but in poor areas, it takes much longer. So, people in those places have to deal with stinky, dirty water for a long time. Jobs can disappear, and that's a big deal for families who depend on those paychecks. This whole cycle can keep going, making things worse. Extreme weather makes people poorer, and being poor makes it harder to handle extreme weather.

Now, about climate change—it's making these crazy weather things happen more often. Think of it like our planet is getting a fever because of all the pollution we're putting in the air. And who's causing most of this pollution? It's usually the richer countries, not the poorer ones. But guess who's getting hit the hardest by this fever? Yep, the poorer countries. It's not fair, is it?

Poorer countries don't have the fancy tools or money to protect themselves from climate change. They didn't cause this problem, but they're suffering the most. It's like someone else making a mess, and you have to clean it up.

In the end, extreme weather and inequality are a big problem. People who don't have much money are getting hit the worst by crazy weather, and it's not their fault. It's time for everyone, especially the rich countries, to help out and make things fairer. We need to reduce pollution, build better houses, and make sure everyone has what they need to stay safe when the weather goes wild. It's the right thing to do.

Untitled
by Larissa Heniger

Money is all that matters in this world. Who cares if you live or die, if you can't pay someone to save you then why would you matter? All of these thoughts hit me with a large crash louder than the sound of roaring thunder. The wind sounded strong too, especially as it rushed to knock me off of my feet. My ears could only focus on the sound of nature going against us, my family shouting out to me being the one thing to snap me out of this realization I was having. The rain changed from pattering to hail and the water level was past my feet, to my ankles. I slodged out my feet to run up to home, but after that, I had nowhere safer to go. The water was getting high in the street and I knew it would soon reach my home.

We used bags of rice to barricade the front door, hoping it would hold from the wind and soak up some of the water. My younger siblings, parents and grandparents all had to try and survive in this small home, yet, this small home is all I have ever known. This home—my home was going to be damaged by a category-4 hurricane and the great flood brought by the rain. But even worse, my home can't guarantee my family safety due to the fact that we can't afford a home built to survive this weather.

In the distance, outside my window, I couldn't help but notice a tree being blown down into someone's home. This helped me realize that this isn't just my family and my home, but my neighborhood.

Do you think on the other side of town that someone is safe and sound? On the other side of town, someone is untouched. Over here, the wind pushes things into our homes and water goes up to our cabinets and counters. But hasn't it always been that way? The land of the free is the land of the rich.

Untitled
by Erin Hollier

I never realized how good I truly had it until it was all gone in the blink of an eye. It was 8 A.M. one summer morning when I was being startled awake by my mom frantically shaking me. In my dazed confusion from having just been woken up, I barely noticed the chaos that was going on around me.

This wasn't the first time something like this happened so we knew to start preparing early but we didn't know it would be this bad. When we heard the news that a hurricane was going to hit in a few days we began to prepare early since we had gotten a few inches of rain in the house a couple times in the past. We prepared by moving anything that was low to the ground up onto higher places such as tables, chairs, and counters. What we didn't expect was that all that preparation would be in vain.

I woke up the morning of to my mom shaking me awake asking me to help her. I was confused at first but after looking down at the floor and seeing more than a foot of water I realized what was happening. My first thought was to make sure that my cat was okay because the night before she had refused to come inside so she spent the night outside. I quickly jumped out of bed and got dressed and ran outside. After calling her name and searching the yard for a few minutes, I eventually found her hiding in the garage. She was shaking from being wet and I quickly scooped her up and brought her inside. After that I started helping my mom and brother pack the necessities. When the water reached about two feet in the house and the roads were still somewhat drivable we decided it best to leave while possible.

We knew other areas were flooding even worse so it was a struggle finding someplace to go. After calling around to a few different relatives in other places we found out that my grandma's house wasn't flooding and the water on the roads was relatively low near her house. After hearing this news we finished packing the truck and left about an hour later. It was an hour and a half drive there but with all the flooding and roads closed it took nearly three hours with the only scenery being flooding buildings and things floating down the road. We eventually got there and quickly rushed inside to avoid getting drenched by the rain still falling. My grandma had two guest rooms so me and my mom stayed in one and my brother stayed in the other. I was glad to be off the road and not having to stand in water up to my waist.

After staying there for about a week we decided to head home once the raining had stopped and the water had gone down. Although our stay there was nice and we were lucky to have somewhere to go, we were anxious to get home and see the damage that we would be having to deal with. We told my grandma we were leaving and packed all our things that night. The next morning we said our goodbyes, loaded the car, and headed out. The ride back home was depressing with all the ruined yards and flooded cars on the sides of roads. We eventually made it home, much faster than when we left, and went inside to take in the damage. Nearly all of the furniture had been ruined and the water had gotten so high after we left that it reached the things on the tables and counters. It was depressing to know that nearly everything we had was ruined and that we would have to basically start over.

This experience, although a great tragedy for many people that experienced it, has taught me to always be prepared for the worst and to never take what I have for granted.

The Connection
by Christopher Johnson

In the tempest's fearful grasp we lie,
Exposing our truths, a stormy sky.
Extreme weather upon us all,
A jarring reminder—nature's call.

Rain and hail, a heavy toll,
It spares not one, rich or poor
Yet the scales of fate unbalanced sway,
Inequality whispers, dark and vague.

Wind and waves fall hard on lands,
Puppeteers in climate change's hands.
A dance untamed, destruction spun,
Reality weaved, but stories unsung.

The privileged shield what's theirs to keep,
While for commoners, inequity seeps.
Basic needs vanish in thin air,
Forgotten struggles, resounding despair.

Amidst the chaos and chilling gale,
We realize disparity prevails.
As currents merge and tears are dried,
Together we stand, side by side.

Bound by vulnerability within the core,
Inequality brings forth a roiling shore.
To nurture Earth with equal hands,
Bridging gaps that divide our lands.

In the face of weather ever extreme,
Dismantling hierarchy must be our dream.
For only then shall we break free,
To build a future of equity.

Untitled
by Aletra Jones

Extreme weather events, such as hurricanes, floods, and heatwaves, can have a significant impact on different communities, and these impacts are often felt more strongly by those who are already facing social and economic disadvantages. This creates a cycle of inequality that further marginalized vulnerable populations.

One way extreme weather events contribute to inequality is through the destruction of infrastructure and property. Marginalized communities often lack the resources and financial means to adequately prepare for or recover from these events. As a result, they may face prolonged periods of displacement, inadequate housing, and limited access to basic services like clean water and electricity.

In addition to the physical damage, extreme weather events can also have long-term health impacts. For example, during heatwaves, individuals without access to air conditioning or living in areas with limited green spaces may be at a higher risk of heat-related illnesses. Similarly, flooding can lead to waterborne diseases and exacerbate existing health disparities in communities with limited access to healthcare.

Economically, extreme weather events can perpetuate inequality by disproportionately affecting livelihoods and exacerbating poverty. For example, farmers who rely on agriculture for their income may face significant crop losses due to droughts or floods, pushing them further into poverty. This economic instability can have long-term consequences for individuals and communities, widening the wealth gap and hindering social mobility.

To address these inequalities, it is crucial to implement policies and initiatives that prioritize the needs of marginalized communities. This includes investing in resilient infrastructure, improving access to affordable housing, healthcare, and education, and ensuring that emergency response and recovery efforts are equitable and inclusive. Additionally, promoting sustainable practices and mitigating climate change can help reduce the frequency and severity of extreme weather events, benefiting all communities.

In conclusion, extreme weather events exacerbate existing inequalities by disproportionately affecting vulnerable populations. By recognizing and addressing these disparities, we can work towards building a more just and resilient society for all.

Untitled

by Jael Jones

Isn't it strange? We hear storms and think of damage, danger even, without a thought, without a reason. We treat lightning and thunder like treason, whilst familiar with weather patterns that change like the seasons, but weather can be peaceful no matter if lightning strikes, weather can be beautiful even if it's scary at night. Isn't It strange? If storms are so dangerous then why do people stay and admire them willingly? Why do people not take storms so seriously? Rain, Sleet, Hail, Snow, it can all be dangerous yet playing around is something we can't outgrow. As kids, adults, we play in snow, no second thought on how it might affect us, We pray and pray and beg for rain knowing we'd hate it to pour onto us, we hate the bad weather, we hate what we can't control, but we love to think when we pray for rain its the power itself we hold. Isn't it strange? How weather can go from light rain to thunder, from a little thunder to lightning, from lightning to extreme winds that turn into a hurricane. Isn't it strange? That when that damage hits after praying for that rain but receiving pain instead of new growth of flowers and grains. Isn't it strange? How we as human beings beg for things to come to us right when we want them but when we get them it's too much, it's not enough. Maybe us singing for this rain to go away, but receiving it anyway is our punishment from God? Mother Nature maybe? All for trying to control what we weren't meant to. A quote from a musical is a motto I now live by; "I am the one thing in life I can control" I follow it without a question as to why, we all should, you only live once so live, right? I as a human know my role, how you choose to own yours is on you and you alone.

Equity in the Eye of the Storm: The Impact of Extreme Weather on Vulnerable Communities
by Ibrahim Khankhail

Hurricanes, which are fires, floods, droughts, and scorching temperatures are growing more common and strong, inflicting substantial harm to individuals, communities, and the natural world. These occurrences are frequently triggered by global warming, that is primarily brought about by human actions such as the use of fossil fuels, deforestation, and industrial farming. However, the consequences of extreme weather events are not dispersed evenly, with underprivileged people generally bearing the brunt of the devastation.

For a variety of reasons, poverty worsens the effects of extreme weather occurrences. For starters, marginalized groups are frequently located in locations more susceptible to catastrophic weather occurrences, such as floodplains, unstable slopes, or low-lying coastal areas. Housing in these locations is frequently substandard and provides little defense from storm or flood damage. Furthermore, vulnerable populations frequently have limited access to insurance, loans, and other financial safeguards that could assist them in recovering from these catastrophes.

Second, poverty makes it more difficult for individuals to plan for and recover from natural disasters. People may not have the resources, for example, to stockpile food and water or move to safer places during a storm. Individuals may not have enough money to reconstruct their homes or replace destroyed items after a catastrophe. In addition, when governments and humanitarian organizations respond to extreme weather disasters, wealthy populations are frequently prioritized over vulnerable communities, leaving the latter to fend for themselves. Third, catastrophic weather events can exacerbate already existing inequities. Because affluent societies are better able to guard and recover from disaster, Hurricanes may force them to grow more isolated and less likely to aid others. This may result in social estrangement and marginalization, as well as a 'every man for himself' culture.

Finally, catastrophic weather events can exacerbate existing social and economic issues. People who cannot afford air conditioning, for example, may suffer from heat exhaustion or dehydration during a heatwave. Farmers with limited access to water may lose crops during a drought, pushing them further into poverty. Extreme weather events may worsen these differences as inequality continues to rise.

Blown Around in the Wind
by Marissa Lang

At some point in life, everyone has had their weak, solemn moments when they feel like the world is beating down on them, the wind is blowing them around, and there is no one to help. They feel hopeless and in need of some calm, shiny day. Southeast Texas has had some pretty horrific times considering its vast history of awful hurricanes and other extreme weather disasters. Along with this, we've recently experienced hurricane Harvey, and although it was very apparent that our area struggled greatly, we never received the amount of help that we truly needed during this disaster.

I still remember the week hurricane Harvey hit. I was going into sixth grade and my first few weeks of school were delayed. Thankfully our house didn't flood but most of my neighbors' homes did and many of our family friends and family members' homes flooded, so our house was packed full. We were stuck making lots of homemade soups, breads and other canned or frozen items for the large group of people we hosted. I was pushed out of my room and my grandparents stayed in there while I uncomfortably slept on a sleeping bag near many of my cousins in the living room. This natural disaster shut down many of our refineries and businesses due to hurricane damage. It took forever for southeast Texas to get up and running and more assistance was needed. With additional outside help, we could have started our lives sooner, but this wasn't the case. We were at the dispense of those civilians and small associations willing to help when they could.

Our areas were drowning in flood waters and disconnected with no electricity or ways of transportation and a lot of communication. Most parts of our small towns were either half way under water or almost blown away, and still, no extra help was given. Priority was the major cities, like Houston and other major cities even though they shouldn't have been higher on the list according to precedence of severity. The government and many rescue associations were not as considerate with help in Southeast Texas as we'd hoped. It is biased to have chosen to help the more well-known towns over the ones with more severity.

Southeast Texas was at a depressing point. Many who lost their cars due to flood waters had no way of transportation. There were also many people who experienced the sad loss of their home and everything inside, there was no way to fight or prevent the growing waters or the thousands of towers and trees that were blown around by the strong and ruthless wind and rain. So many were devastated and although our town was able to recover within a few months, many who never saw their lost pets again, who lost their prized possessions, or everything in their life, took much longer to recover. Many lives changed due to the lack of assistance we had and the strong and damaging hurricane.

Southeast Texas has suffered in so many ways due to the unbelievable hurricanes and weather conditions and the combined recovery time that isn't shortened because of the inequality our area receives. We have the lower hand in public help and have struggled against fighting for help against bigger cities for so long. Everyone deserves help, not just those in largely populated areas, everyone deserves to be on the priority list and not shoved aside.

Untitled
by Aiden Le

Life is not this perfectly smooth road where there may be bumps and cracks that come with it. People face problems and overcome obstacles each and every day. Weather is a major cause of problems in people's lives. People fear and begin to panic when the idea of extreme weather rises. Extreme weather is unpredictable and can not be avoided. Texas has dealt with many types of extreme weather, such as hurricanes and tropical storms. In recent times, Southeast Texas was filled with fear from Hurricane Harvey and Tropical Storm Imelda.

In the year of 2017, Texans began hearing about this hurricane that is developing, known as Hurricane Harvey. People realized how dangerous this hurricane was forming and started to become worried. The media was being flooded with updates on the development of Hurricane Harvey, and I also became concerned. I remember my family was always watching the news for new updates and information. My family was always informing me about the hurricane and it felt like the hurricane was becoming more and more severe. Hurricane Harvey ended up reaching the gulf coast area and was predicted to affect where I live. The stress in my family began to rise as Hurricane Harvey was headed our way. Hurricane Harvey was expected to come in effect at any time, and the communities in my area were preparing quickly for this hurricane. My parents prepared by gathering a lot of essential food and sandbags to block the water from seeping into the house. The devastation of Hurricane Harvey began. Hurricane Harvey was in effect, and the rain seemed to constantly pour down heavily, filling all the area around me with water. In the midst of extreme weather, my family and I were trapped in our house, as we watched the water keep rising to higher levels. We put out sandbags to possibly keep the water from coming in. The water soon started to reach our garage, and we were really afraid of the water getting into our house. Sandbags began to fill with water and no longer could prevent the water from going further. My parents realized that there was nothing we could do but let our house get filled with water. The water creeped from all the sides of our house. The walls of my house began absorbing up with water, and water began creeping onto the floor of my house. All of our belongings were being flooded and submerged in the water. While our house is being flooded with water, the rain keeps on falling, and my family and I are isolated in the upstairs of our house. At that time, the water reached levels that were right below my knee. My family and I were traumatized as we watched from the upstairs of our house while our downstairs got filled with flood water. The streets of Southeast Texas and houses surrounding them were flooded with water. We experienced a total of 36 hours of heavy rainfall causing water to continuously rise. Southeast Texas reached a total of 60 inches of rain, and my house was flooded with a total of 12 inches of rain. When Hurricane Harvey was slowing down and finally coming to an end, families patiently waited for the rain to recede so we could see the aftermath of this devastating event. My family lost the majority of our belongings due to the flood, and our house was ruined. We had to tear down the walls and floors of our house that was affected by the flood. Hurricane Harvey drastically affected our lives. We had to completely renovate the bottom half of our house while our family of 8 stayed in a one bedroom living area. My family had to adjust to a new lifestyle due to Hurricane Harvey.

A couple years later, there was another storm that would potentially cause a similar effect like Hurricane Harvey did. My family just finished rebuilding the downstairs of our home. We fully remodeled our kitchen, bedroom, bathroom, living room, floor, and walls of our house. My family was nervous of any form of extreme weather due to the tragedy Hurricane Harvey had on us. We were alerted that Tropical Storm Imelda was headed our way, so we had to prepare for another storm. Our preparation for Imelda was similar to Hurricane Harvey. This was now our second time having to deal with extreme weather. We had recently bought a lot of new furniture for our house due to losing our furniture during Hurricane Harvey. My parents put our furniture on stands to elevate it off the ground, so they possibly won't get affected by the flood. Suddenly, Tropical Storm Imelda hit, and Southeast Texas is facing another storm. Imelda was very stressful for the people of Southeast Texas. The feeling was unreal, as it felt like we were dealing with Hurricane Harvey all over again. The sound of rain or thunderstorms brought fear to my family. The idea of our house flooding again frightened us. The rain continued to fall down and water kept rising. Soon, our house was flooded for the second time. We had to repeat the same demolition and rebuilding process of our home identical to Hurricane Harvey. Extreme weather has drastically affected our lives.

Extreme weather has caused serious challenges in people's lives, but weather can not be tolerated. The topic of extreme weather can not be ignored as it is a frequent problem in our lives. Weather is very unfortunate due to the fact it can't be controlled. Overall, people have to persevere and overcome the obstacles extreme weather may bring to them.

Extreme Weather & Inequality
by Ayonna Lewis

I have never seen houses swallowed up by the streets or parts of houses scattered in neglected places. Things that should be inside somehow find their way onto the slide at a nearby park. Hurricane Harvey was the first hurricane I saw with my own eyes this week. Something happened every day. This long week has been terrible for the eyes. I could imagine what would be worse than that. Other extreme weather events such as tornadoes, frost and floods also occur worldwide.

I was in Houston, Texas at the time of the event, where the beginning was just beginning and alerts were being broadcast through televisions, telephones and other electronic devices. The buzzing sound that constantly rang in your ears, you could hear it even when it wasn't playing. On the first day, stores were destroyed to gather resources needed to deal with the natural disaster. Parents with children looking for essentials and older adults getting help pushing and shoving their frail bodies. Then it was time for everyone to get in and stay indoors as the sky no longer showed its natural colors and storm clouds quickly formed. Power lines are snapped in half, trees invade surrounding homes and stray animals seek shelter. The wind increased so much that objects were thrown through the sky, also causing damage. While we tried to keep everyone entertained, we played various games to keep your teens' minds from wandering. I looked out the window every few hours to see if there were any signs that it was over. Inside the house you could hear the heavy rain hailing and cold temperatures seeping in from under the door.

Hurricane Harvey is one of the worst hurricanes to hit the United States in recent memory, ranking 10th on the list of worst hurricanes in American history. The storm caused an estimated $155 billion in damage and destroyed or damaged approximately 178,000 structures. Millions have been spent since the storm to rebuild homes and infrastructure, while other funds have been used to reduce flooding and improve drainage. According to Judge Branick, the City of Port Authority's emergency operations center's phone lines were overloaded, so they began rolling over into the operations center. Since the hurricane, homes have been constructed much higher than before the storm. The county's main focus since the storm has been on flood prevention and mitigation. In addition to hurricanes, the county has also experienced drought and flooding. During the 2021 drought, there were exceptional and widespread losses of crops and pasture, as well as extreme fire risks, resulting in water emergencies.

The effects of Hurricane Harvey on individuals have been far-reaching, with 43% of losses resulting from property damage, the highest rate of occurrence among other natural disasters in the Greater Houston area since 2004. Ethnic-based minorities were particularly impacted by the storm and its aftermath, with many losing their homes, relocating to shelters, and losing valuable possessions. The Red Cross responded to the disaster by providing $45 million in emergency assistance to over 100,000 people, deploying over 3,000 personnel and volunteers, deploying 171 rescue vehicles, providing 965 million meals and snacks, and operating shelters in the affected counties. Additionally, the social impact of the disaster has been severe, with 10,000 individuals trapped inside or flooded highways, and many relocating to temporary housing. As a result of these events, many communities, including mine, have responded by donating food and necessities to the closest churches and foundations in the affected areas.

People in lower-middle-income countries are about five times more likely to be displaced by sudden extreme weather disasters than people in high-income countries. Traditionally marginalized communities are the hardest hit and most impacted. In other societies, women and men living in poverty had to explore to obtain resources and things to consume, increasing the risk of violence from others. For example, survival of the fittest when there is a lack of demand for all and limited supply for all leads to a shortage of leasing on the black market.

What we can do together as a community is to develop a more sustainable commute, produce more shelf-stable food locally, and reduce energy use in buildings. Greater communication by communities can help prepare everyone for drastic climate change. This would give them more time to plan more efficiently. The shelf-stable foods can be stored for a long period of time and will not run out easily if you have to stay isolated until the climate is suitable. Reducing electricity consumption in buildings could help store energy, and power would not go out as quickly during severe weather. Cities should invest money in more organizations and insurance against future disasters to be better prepared.

Our Journey Towards Resolving Extreme Weather Inequalities
by Crystal Liu

In our homely city of Beaumont, Texas, an area known for its resiliency against natural disasters, extreme weather and inequality plays out against the backdrop of the Piney Woods and the Gulf of Mexico. Extreme weather events have revealed to us the true harshness of inequality and the disparities that lie within our community. When the most destructive hurricanes or deadly heat waves hit, our community's most vulnerable are the most adversely impacted.

It is the families living paycheck to paycheck, struggling to afford flood insurance, who must endure the heart-wrenching experience of watching their homes and livelihoods wash away. It is the children living in areas of lower socioeconomic status, whose school is closed due to extreme flooding, facing uncertainty about school displacement and their future education. It is our beloved seniors who are immobilized and trapped by the debris of their homes after the storm. It is the highway worker, making ends meet for his family, who must withstand the scorching beams of sun on his back during long work hours as global temperatures steadily rise. It is the marginalized communities, often relegated to areas plagued by pollution and industrial waste, who are put into situations of environmental injustice when disaster strikes. In our community, these disparities are evident, and it's a reality that we must no longer ignore.

But today, as our city acknowledges these stark realities, we must also recognize the power within our community, starting with our youth. There's a group of passionate individuals in Beaumont, which I am a part of, at West Brook High School's Green Club who are committed to promoting environmental sustainability through taking action at the school and community level, recognizing inequalities caused by extreme weather, and being ready to act when disaster strikes next. We intend to fulfill our mission which is our motto: service to the earth, and service to a sustainable future. Our humble club is taking on a monumental mission, but we believe in the power of one step at a time.

A large part of our mission is our monthly campus cleanups. With trash bags and determination, we scour every crevice of our school grounds. We pick up litter and restore our school's natural beauty. It is a simple act, but a clear message is sent: we are the change-makers and we care deeply about our environment.

In the spring, school gardening becomes our next endeavor. Together, we planted a vibrant fig tree. As the tree grows larger and sturdier, our sense of pride and accomplishment grows with it. Inspired by our success with our tree, we plan to further our gardening endeavors as a life-skill learning opportunity for the special education department and an act of goodwill to the community, as we will be harvesting the crops in the fall and donating them to the local soup kitchen.

Another major part of our mission is our school's recycling program. We believe that every bottle and every can has the potential to make a difference, and we recognize that many of our city's residents have a lack of access to the sustainable option of recycling. Currently, we educate our peers on the importance of recycling and the inaccessibility to it some residents face, set up bins in strategic locations, and diligently sort materials with Lamar University's Green Squad and ExxonMobil's Environmental Awareness Sustainability Team every first Saturday of the month at Lamar University. Over the years, our school's recycling program has witnessed significant growth, with an increasing number of high school students actively participating and engaging in our school's and community's recycling initiatives.

Finally, at the very core of our mission lies our desire to educate our peers. This year, Green Club officers are making efforts to research environmental topics to present to the club. Being aware and educated is the first step in constructing any action plan, and in order to create a generation that fights for today's and tomorrow's earth, we must do our duty of sowing in the seeds of knowledge that grow into meaningful action.

Though we have no direct experience with mitigating the damage of extreme weather, our current actions to promote sustainability and educate others are building a foundation of an environmentally conscious character and resiliency to address the inequalities from extreme weather in the future. We are creating changes in both our characters and community, one step at a time. Our cleanups, gardening, recycling initiatives, and educational campaigns are like drops in an ocean, but together, they are forming ripples of transformation today and for the future to come. The small steps we take now are building a sustainable legacy for our school and community as well as inspiring others to join our cause now and in the future.

So, whether it's a regular, weekly cleanup; the joy of watching our tree grow; the simple act of recycling; or an informational seminar, our Green Club is proof that positive changes are possible through tiny steps. When we are in the face of extreme weather and inequality in the future, let us be the voice for those who are unheard and the hand that reaches out to lift others up. With our current foundation being built, it is within our power to close the gap, to stand up for environmental justice, and to ensure that no one is left behind when the next storm comes. With passion, dedication, and a shared vision, we are shaping a greener, more equal future for all. And we're doing it one small, meaningful action at a time.

Screams
by Abril Lopez

For the winds scream as if it was kids crying
The currents rise as the sun has fallen by clouds
And the day is covered in darkness

Moms worried about their homes
Dads worried about their cars
Kids worried about their playgrounds
For they fear the scream will wipe their home
With no money to get them out they must stay put

For the clouds start to eat their crops
For they hope their home isn't next
For all they can do is hope for the clumps of air to calm
For the tornado has taken over their home

Climas Extremos y Desigualdad/
Extreme Weather and Inequality
por/by Adithleidy Lopez-Magallon

An English translation follows the original Spanish

Cuando se piensa en climas extremos, se recuerda lo mal que la pasamos, pero sugaramente muy poca gente reflexiona sobre las personas que tenían pocos recursos y se quedaron sin nada, ante un desastre natural. En condiciones climátacas severas, algunas personas pueden experimentar desigualdad, debido a la falta recursos básicos como agua, alimentos y el no tener acceso a la transportacíon para evacuar a un lugar seguro.

Los eventos extremos más comunes en el Sureste de Tejas son los huracanes. Durante estos desastres naturales, las personas que carecen de necesidades esenciales pueden enfrentar desafíos significativos. Cuando las familias del Sureste de Tejas son notificadas que un huracán se aproxima el área, la primera cosa que hacen es abastecerse con cosas para la supervivencia, como agua y comida. De acuerdo a la téoria de jerarquía de necesidades de Abraham Maslow, propone que las personas se rigen por cinco categorías de necesidades básicas: fisiológicas, seguridad, amor, estima y autorrealización. Según Maslow, el nivel que se considera lo más primordial son las necesidades fisiológicas; sin embargo personas de bajo ingreso sufren de desigualdad por no poder obtener estos elementos indispensables. Es esencial abordar estas desigualdades y garantizar que todos tengan acceso a los recursos necesarios para sobrevivir y mantenerse seguros en climas extremos. Una forma de ayudar a estas personas a tener la posibilidad de adquirir necesidades primarias es estableciendo lugares donde personas con dificultades económicas puedan recibir estas cosas de forma gratuita. Durante el huracán Harvey, muchas organizaciones crearon sitios donde regalaban recursos básicos para estas personas desfavorecidas.

Siguiendo la jerarquía de Maslow la segunda categoría es la seguridad, que puede ser amenazada al no tener modos de transportación. No tener acceso a transporte durante climas extremos puede crear desigualdad porque limita la capacidad de la personas para protegerse y ponerse a salvo durante situaciones de emergencia. Sin movilidad para crear un plan de evacuación claro y accesible, algunas personas pueden tener dificultades para encontrar refugio seguro o recibir ayuda adecuada durante desastres naturales. Por consecuente, esto implica un mayor riesgo para la vida y bienestar de personas menos privilegiadas en comparación con aquellos que tienen acceso a recursos económicos, apoyo y transportación. Es importante garantizar que todos tengan acceso a medios necesarios para evacuar de manera segura en climas extremos y así reducir las desigualdades ante una emergencia. Usando el ejemplo de Harvey nuevamente, vimos como nuestra comunidad se unió para rescatar a personas en situación de vulnerabilidad.

Es esencial reconocer que en situaciones de clima extremo, las personas que carecen de recursos básicos como agua, alimentos y transporte pueden ser víctimas de la desigualdad. Pero es inspirador ver cómo nuestra comunidad se une para combatir estas desigualdades y ayudar a quienes más lo necesitan.

When we think about extreme weather, our focus often centers on our own negative experiences. However, seldom do we pause to consider those who had few resources and find themselves with nothing in the wake of a natural disaster. Some people may face inequality during severe weather conditions due to the lack of basic resources such as water and food, and lack of access to transportation to be ableto evacuate to a safe place.

In Southeast Texas, hurricanes are the most prevalent extreme weather event. During these natural disasters, people who lack essential resources can encounter significant challenges. When families in Southeast Texas receive notifications of an approaching hurricane, the first thing they do is to obtain vital survival items such as water and food. Abraham Maslow's hierarchy of needs theory identifies five fundamental categories that people are governed by: physiological, safety, love, esteem, and self-realization. According to Maslow, needs at the physiological level are considered primary; nevertheless, individuals with low incomes face inequality as they struggle to acquire these indispensable elements. It is imperative to address these inequalities and ensure that everyone has access to the resources needed to survive and remain safe during extreme weather events. One effective approach to giving people the opportunity to meet essential needs is to establish sites where those facing financial difficulties can obtain needed items free of charge. During Hurricane Harvey, numerous organizations set up sites to give basic resources to disadvantaged individuals.

Following Maslow's hierarchy, the second category is safety, which can be compromised by a lack of transportation. The absence of transportation during extreme weather events can create inequality by restricting people's abilities to safeguard themselves and reach safety during emergencies. Lack of transportation hinders the creation of a clear and accessible evacuation plan, making it challenging for some individuals to find safe shelter or receive adequate aid during natural disasters. As a result, this poses a greater risk to the life and well-being of less privileged individuals, compared to those with access to financial resources, support, and transportation. It is important to ensure that everyone has access to the necessary resources for a safe evacuation during extreme weather events, thereby reducing inequalities in the face of emergencies. In the example of Hurricane Harvey, we saw our community come together to rescue individuals in vulnerable situations.

It is essential to acknowledge that during extreme weather events, individuals without basic resources such as water, food, and transportation become susceptible to inequality. Nevertheless, it is inspiring to witness our community coming together to address these inequalities and assist those who are most in need.

English translation by Dania Santana

Tyler's Storm
by Matthew Lou

"There she goes! What a magnificent sight! The Extra EA-300 soaring through the sky, twirling and spinning. How the pilot doesn't get dizzy, I have no idea."

I stare intently at the television, absorbed in watching the airshow. Tingles run down my spine and I get goosebumps all over. It's not that I've never seen an airshow before, but I've noticed that something inside me gets sparked each time I see a plane.

Most of my friends tell me that they're still not really sure what they want to do with their life. They're heading off to college or trade school, but really that's just another placeholder in their life. Me? I'm all set. I know exactly where I'm going.

"I'm going to be a pilot," I announce aloud, still drooling over the planes flying back and forth over the TV.

"Tyler, can you shut up?" my sister says from the other side of the room. She looks like she's doing her homework, which is honestly really surprising, for her. Maybe she's failed a little too many classes.

"I'm telling you, Keira, you're gonna miss me when I'm gone."

"I don't think so."

"Ah, but if I'm gone, then you'll have more to eat! I feel bad for making mom and dad go to the food bank all the time."

"Can you, like, leave?"

I consider it for a moment, and head over to the door. I was in the mood for a walk anyway, and annoying my sister is something I've done so much over the years; maybe I can let her off the hook for now.

I turn the knob to our weathered door and step outside. It's just barely sprinkling, so it must not be that big of a deal if I don't go back inside for an umbrella. I walk into the rain and once the raindrops start hitting me, I feel as if I've become one with nature.

It's as if they're piercing me—washing the impurities out of my soul. Suddenly, I'm very sad. I just remembered that this will be the last time I get to feel the rain like this. Where I live, it's very humid and it rains a lot. I've always complained about it. "Mosquitoes suck!" "The weather sucks!" It was only till my days here in this beloved town were numbered did I realize that this could be something that I will miss.

Before long the rain is not just sprinkling. It's hitting me hard. The rain is falling very strangely. I'm not sure why, but something feels off. The wind is blowing way harder than normal, and the rain just feels plain weird. I rush back into my house right as the thunder starts to rumble. I step over to the window and see the sky light up with a crack of lightning.

"You're back? I was hoping you got blown away," Keira says flatly. I laugh, sitting across from her at the table she's working at.

"The storm is really strong right now. Is there a hurricane or something?"

Keira looks at me like I'm stupid, which is valid, since I think I am admittedly pretty stupid.

"There is a hurricane. Have you not been watching the weather? The news? TV? Anything?"

I reply, "Well, I don't really pay attention to that stuff. And the power is out half the time, 'cause we can't pay the electrical bills. You know that already."

"When are you going to go to that pilot school or whatever already?"

I clear my throat dramatically, "Actually, it's called aviation school. And I'm supposed to leave tomorrow, but it's probably gonna be delayed for a bit thanks to this weather."

She doesn't reply, most likely already bored with the conversation.

In the silence that follows, a crack of thunder makes me jump. My heart starts beating wildly. My brain is telling me something. Something important. I need to do something.

"Keira!" I shout, standing up immediately. I don't know what has possessed me, but my voice is filled with a vigor I've never felt before.

"What?"

"Get under the table. Now!"

Normally, she never agrees with anything I say, but the urgency in my voice seems to get across, and she complies. She ducks under the table calmly.

For a moment, I thought about warning my parents, but I remember that they're still at work. Even though they wanted to, they never could afford to get a day off even in such violent weather conditions. I can only hope that they get to safety. *Safety from what?* I wonder, still not sure why my instincts tell me that something bad is going to happen.

I crawl under the table with Keira. Not even a few seconds after I'm safe under the table, the power goes off, and we're thrown into darkness. The whirr of the AC and the quiet muttering of the TV abruptly stop. The power is out again. All that's left is the raging sound of the storm.

I hear an ominous crack. Is it a tree? A house? What just happened?

The lightning flashes, lighting up the dark house for a moment. The thunder quickly follows. I can feel Keira grip my arm, but I barely notice—I'm scared stiff myself.

Another ominous crack.

Then the house shakes, as if a giant brought his fist down on the roof with all his force. Outside, I can hear the wind howling and screaming. The sounds only intensify.

Keira starts sobbing, and I hug her tightly. If I were by myself, I would probably pass out from the fear. But I have to stay strong. Stay strong, at least for her.

The loud crack again.

Then, the world collapses.

Concrete and wood crash all over the floor. The roof is totaled. Rain starts to fall in. In the middle of it all, a tree is laid horizontally where our roof used to be.

I'm so shocked that I don't even scream. I don't even move. I just stare. Staring at the darkness. At the unknown. I'm always staring, even with the planes. I've never touched a plane before, but I always wished I could. I never wanted the house to be destroyed by a falling tree, but I wished I could stop it.

It's almost as if nature itself is accusing me of my inaction. I always brag about knowing what I want to be, but have I really ever *done* what I want to be? What good is a dream if all you do is dream of it?

The water starts to leak into our little shelter under the table, but I don't care. I only wish for this nightmare to end. Wish, wish, wish. That's all I've ever done.

Maybe one day, I can finally *do* . . .

"Thank you so much for your help, young man," says one of the people helping out with restoration, "What was your name, again?"

"Tyler," I say, shaking his hand firmly, "Glad to help."

"I understand this isn't even your home. I'm sure a handsome, healthy young man like yourself has other things to do, do you not?"

I laugh. He's not wrong.

"I don't know. I just really felt like helping out, I guess?"

I'm not doing it for recognition. I'm not doing it for money, for volunteer hours, or anything physical like that. I want to help, just to help.

I see a toy airplane on the floor, and can't help but laugh as I pick it up. Who knows where it flew in from? It reminds me of my own dream—to eventually take flight.

Sometimes, when I'm feeling down, I remember the disaster that happened when the hurricane trashed my family's home. The money that I planned to use for my new life, learning to be a pilot, was voluntarily given to my family to repair the house. Our family was already in a precarious financial situation, so I wasn't really in a position to just leave them. When I'm in a bad mood, I tell myself it's the hurricane's fault. I tell myself that the hurricane destroyed my dream. That it's unfair. Why can other people do what they like just because they have money? What did I do to deserve this? I tell myself it's everyone and everything else's fault.

But realistically, it was more like my wake-up call.

Maybe I'm not a pilot now, but I have all my life to pursue that dream. For now, I'll start slow. I'll go at my own pace. My community is more important to me, so I'd much rather cherish that than a fleeting dream. You can't choose what life you're born into, but you can choose what life you will live. As I wipe the hard-earned sweat from my forehead, I smile, looking up at the clear sky that I will one day conquer.

And next time, not even a hurricane will stop me.

A Story of Hurricanes, Trailer Parks, and Hope
by Jamie Lyles

"Trailer park trash." In the world of preconceived judgments, this term resonates as a stark reminder of stereotypes and societal biases. This derogatory phrase once hurled my way after my family's relocation to an R.V. park, speaks volumes about the unspoken challenges we faced. Unwanted but unyielding, we found ourselves in this situation due to economic turmoil. In the midst of inflation's relentless surge and plummeting economy, my mother lost her job, and we faced the grim reality of losing our home. This ultimately led us to find a new home located within the confines of a trailer park. As the words of my fellow students stung, I gathered my inner strength and masked the hurt with a brave face. Life, though far from ideal, was still manageable. However, this equilibrium was shattered by the unrelenting force of Hurricane Rita, the first extreme weather disaster we would have to endure.

I knew it was going to be bad when the mandatory evacuation was called. My mother loaded us up with a few snacks and drinks, and we hit the road thinking we could make it to Lufkin in a few hours. Instead, we were met with almost stand-still traffic, and our gas indicator arrow slowly headed toward empty. After seven hours, the car died, and we were officially out of gas. Some fellow travelers helped push the car to the side of the road, and that is where we stayed for the next ten hours. We were miserable. It was hot, we had very little food and water, and there was no gas station in sight. Eventually, a policeman brought us five gallons of gas, and we were back on the road for another six hours of driving until finally reaching our destination. A hotel room was home for the next seven days. The next week, as we slowly headed back to our town, the anticipation and nerves of what we would find hit us hard. As we approached the row of large brick homes in the center of town, we saw a group of people sitting in lawn chairs having a cookout amongst the loud hum of generators. There were some branches on the ground but the houses seemed to have minimal damage. I got my hopes up thinking maybe it was not as bad as I thought, but instead, the reality aligned with our anxious apprehension. If you have ever watched the news after an extreme weather event, you would know trailer parks do not fare well. Our trailer was knocked off the cinder block foundation and our roof ripped off. We had nothing but a few clothes and kitchen items that were soaked with musty rain and sewer water. The entire park was devastated with bits and pieces of our neighbors' homes dotting the land. For a child, one of the worst things to see is your mother breaking down in tears because she was at a complete loss of what to do next. After a couple months of staying with different people, as we could no longer wait on government disaster assistance, we found a rent-to-own home that was affordable. It was nice having a house. I was happy.

However, happiness is often short-lived. It's the ebb and flow of the universe, and I was caught in the washout. Another storm was coming. The storm was called Tropical Storm Harvey, and devastating flood waters were relentlessly dumped onto our area. Over fifty inches of rain fell and overwhelmed the city's drainage system. Water crept ever so closely to our home and eventually started pouring in our back door until the entire house had one foot of water in it. My only thought was, "Why us? Why is this happening again? What are we going to do now?" This go-around, my mother did not cry. She told me that everything would be fine, and we would get the mess cleaned up once the water receded. Together we did just that. We ripped out carpet, cut out sheetrock, and mopped and mopped again. We lived in the house with no repairs for another year. There was no extra money for remodeling, and I honestly did not mind as long as we got to stay.

In subsequent years, we have weathered Hurricane Delta, Laura, and an ice storm that caused the electrical grid in Texas to completely fail. It was safeguarded for extreme heat but not an ice storm. Many lower income people were displaced once again. They turned to federal aid, but FEMA could not get to everyone as quickly as they needed help. In my opinion, after living through this very issue, a critical area in need of reform is FEMA assistance. Despite its vital role in disaster recovery, the agency faces persistent issues. Delays in approving FEMA trailers and obstacles related to utility permits and hookups have left many victims waiting for months, stranded in dire conditions. Additionally, there was another issue of placing FEMA trailers in flood zoned areas, which was soon followed by the need to relocate them. These challenges underscore the urgency of enhancing FEMA assistance to ensure more efficient and timely aid to people who are in dire need after catastrophic weather.

Having weathered many extreme weather events in my lifetime, I have come to realize the disproportionate impact these disasters have on lower-income and socioeconomically disadvantaged communities. We did not have insurance because it was not an affordable option, and the government programs did not cover much of our loss. A few ideas I have thought of to help in these situations are first, have a supply of water on hand, ready-to-eat meals, and an immediate place for residents if they are unable to evacuate.

Having these plans in place could help people during the first day while waiting on further supplies, especially if roads in and out of the community are flooded. I also believe before an evacuation is called, fuel trucks should be dispatched to certain locations along the evacuation routes.

Some of these areas are rural and do not have gas stations on every corner. Furthermore, there needs to be a way to repair homes for people who do not have the financial means after the storm. Cutting out the sheetrock that was already molding was not easy, and it took us a very long time. After talking with other storm survivors, costly repairs were a big reason that lower-income families had to relocate or seek shelter in different towns. It is less of a financial burden to leave and start over somewhere new.

As climate change exacerbates the frequency and intensity of extreme weather events, the need for prompt and effective FEMA assistance has become increasingly critical. My experiences have taught me that the struggle is real, and the struggle is even harder without financial stability. I am profoundly grateful for a determined mother who navigated these storms and ensured I had the privilege of a safe and secure environment after each storm. I hope in the future, officials would be able to implement disaster relief that helps the low-income community in a quick and more efficient fashion.

Summer Dies in December
by Olivia de la Madrid

The moon
An orb of placid somnolence
Does not quell
The fiery embrace of the sun

Dry, aching, and cracked
The soil begrudgingly
Releases its roots
And parts ways with life

The farmer and his cattle wait
Tongues outstretched for holy wine

Darkness shrouds
The earth releases a sigh
Statis returns
Momentarily

The Ark will not come
Not this time

The tattoo of rain
Burns away any remnant of hope
Flooding the desperate terrain
Flooding the chambers of the heart

Now sliding into the soul
The rain permeates all
Effacing any remnant
Of previous existence

It is November
And he meets
The scalding kiss of death
Surrounded by swollen, floating cattle

Extreme Weather and Inequality
by Ryan Makelki

Throughout history, the lower classes have lived in the less desirable parts of the world. In the modern day, they often live in the regions that are more heavily affected by extreme weather. This is true for both the United States and the world as a whole. This increases their likelihood of having to pay more in repair costs. Climate change also is putting pressure on these areas. The wealthier parts of the world should do what they can to help prevent the damage or fix the effects of extreme weather.

To research this topic, I gathered data on the wealth of the areas of the world affected by extreme weather, and I repeated that process for The United States. I also analyzed how much extreme weather affects monetarily, in both tangible and intangible ways. Furthermore, I investigated how climate change and rising sea levels are affecting this disparity. I limited my research to cyclone-related weather events, due to their widespread impacts. I only used the examples of two countries outside America. In the US, I had to omit the second most hurricane stricken state of Texas, due to its significant amount of land located far enough inland to not be affected by hurricanes.

According to the World Bank, "Compared to their wealthier counterparts, poor people are more likely to live in fragile housing in disaster-prone areas" throughout the world. (Breaking The Link). The historically least wealthy nations often have frequent natural disasters. One example of this is Bangladesh. It has a GDP per capita of only $2,700 compared to the world's average of $21,000 and has a historically harsh monsoon season (GDP Per Capita). From June to October every year, warm moist air from the Indian Ocean delivers significant amounts of rainfall and wind to Bangladesh's coastline. These floods cost Bangladesh $3 billion annually, or about 7% of its national budget (Bangladesh). These monetary figures also do not account for the loss of life and prevention of growth also suffered. The damage suffered by Bangladesh is also felt similarly by numerous other disadvantaged places around the globe. By contrast, Germany only spends €6.6 billion, which is equivalent to $6.97 billion, or 1.4% of its national budget on extreme weather (Kyllmann). This means that the vastly wealthier country of Germany is spending one fifth as much of its budget on extreme weather.

Even in the United States, this pattern of inequality persists. The poverty rate of Mississippi, 18.1%, and Louisiana, 17.2%, are the highest in the nation, and in Florida, it is 12.7%, compared to the national average of 11.2% (Top 10 Poorest States; Poverty rate). Due to their locations, these three states are highly prone to being hit by hurricanes and other tropical cyclones, which cause the most damage per year in the United States compared to any other natural disaster. Since 1851, Florida has been hit by 120 hurricanes, the most out of any state, Louisiana has been hit by 54 hurricanes, and Mississippi has been hit by 19 (Heil). This is made more stark by the fact that only 292 hurricanes have hit the United states as a whole, meaning Florida has had 42% of all hurricanes that hit America (Heil). These states are disproportionately more poverty stricken and hurricane prone than the rest of the country.

The effects of climate change could also be making this inequality worse. Estimates show "that an additional 68 to 135 million people could be pushed into poverty by 2030 because of climate change" (Guivarch et al.). Rising sea levels across the globe are threatening to wipe out millions of homes if nothing is done to combat them. This also disproportionately affects the poorest countries on the planet. However, the policies required to stem the effects of climate change may prove too burdensome for the nations most affected by it. If these nations do nothing about the rising sea levels, millions will be displaced, but if they do spend enough money to combat rising sea levels, they risk pushing more people into poverty with overbearing taxes and neglecting their county's other needs, such as in education. Therefore, "climate change risks both increasing existing economic inequalities and causing people to fall into poverty" if no outside help is given to these poorer areas (Guivarch et al.).

Throughout the United States and the rest of the world, poorer people live in the areas that are most likely to be hit by extreme weather events. This causes them to spend more money on repair costs and limits their possible growth while the wealthier places spend comparatively less. Climate change also plays a factor, forcing countries to have to choose whether to stop rising sea levels by spending more than they can afford, or let the sea destroy millions of people's homes. The richest parts of the world are often the least affected by extreme weather and can continue growing while the poorer parts stagnate. They also have the ability to help the rest of the world prevent the damage of extreme weather or fix its effects, so that they may achieve the same level of growth. Therefore, they have a humanitarian obligation to aid them and reduce inequality.

Works Cited

"Bangladesh: Protect People Most at Risk During Monsoon Season." *Human Rights Watch*, 19 June 2023, www.hrw.org/news/2023/06/19/bangladesh-protect-people-most-risk-during-monsoon-season

"Breaking the Link Between Extreme Weather and Extreme Poverty." *The World Bank,* 14 Nov. 2016, www.worldbank.org/en/news/feature/2016/11/14/breaking-the-link-between-extreme-weather-and-extreme-poverty.

"GDP Per Capita." *Worldometer,* www.worldometers.info/gdp/gdp-per-capita. Accessed 9 Oct. 2023.

Guivarch, Céline, et al. "Linking Climate and Inequality." *International Monetary Fund*, Sep. 2021, www.imf.org/en/Publications/fandd/issues/2021/09/climate-change-and-inequality-guivarch-mejean-taconet.

Heil, Jarrod. "10 U.S. States Where Hurricanes Hit Most Often." *Universal Property,* universalproperty.com/united-states-where-hurricanes-hit-most. Accessed 10 Oct. 2023.

Kyllmann, Carolina. "Germany Still Struggling to Truly Mainstream Climate Adaptation." *Clean Energy Wire*, 13 Apr. 2023, www.cleanenergywire.org/news/germany-still-struggling-truly-mainstream-climate-adaptation.

"Poverty Rate in Florida in the United States From 2000 to 2022." *Statista,* 4 Oct. 2023, www.statista.com/statistics/205451/poverty-rate-in-florida

"Top 10 Poorest States in the U.S." *Friends Committee on National Legislation*, 11 Oct. 2022, www.fcnl.org/updates/2022-10/top-10-poorest-states-us.

Surviving Hurricane Harvey:
A Ten-Year-Old's Perspective
by Leydi Mariel Mascareno

In the summer of 2017, a life-altering tragedy descended upon my family. I was just a ten-year old fifth-grader, eagerly anticipating the return to my elementary school, where the past two years had been filled with friendships, laughter. The school was a place where my friends, cousins, and siblings all learned side by side, creating a close-knit community I cherished. The promise of another school year shone brightly on the horizon. Little did I know, fate had a different path in mind.

I grew up in a low-income household, and my family had only been in the USA for two years. I hadn't encountered a hurricane until Hurricane Harvey came along. At the age of ten, I couldn't fully grasp the gravity of the situation, and neither could my mom, who had experienced milder hurricanes in the past but never in the USA. While I was born in the United States, I was raised in my mother's home country of Honduras, and the English was still a bit difficult to me; we didn't grasp the seriousness of the Hurricane.

When Hurricane Harvey hit Port Arthur, it was nighttime, and we were sound asleep, blissfully unaware. We thought it wouldn't be a severe hurricane and that Houston would bear the brunt of it. However, that night, my mother was jolted awake by loud noises and people outside urgently shouting for everyone to evacuate. She rushed to wake me and my little brother. As I groggily opened my eyes, I could see the fear in her face, and it dawned on me what was happening. It was only 4 a.m., and my mind was still foggy, but a survival instinct kicked in. We had just a few minutes to gather some essentials: a change of clothes and a pair of shoes. I remember wading through water, feeling cold and wet, my small stature barely above the rising flood. I was terrified, imagining snakes or other creatures lurking in the water. My mom, carrying my three-year-old brother on her shoulder, was our guiding light through the chaos.

We left our flooded apartment, we ventured outside and witnessed our neighbors frantically knocking on doors, trying to rouse others as the water levels surged. We climbed the stairs to my uncle's apartment, who lived in the building next to ours. We banged on his door, tears streaming down my face, shivering from the cold and fear. As the hurricane's fury raged outside, my mother was in the grip of sheer terror. I had never witnessed her so vulnerable, so overcome with fear. In that moment, I saw a side of her I had never seen before. Her tears flowed, and her entire being trembled. I couldn't help but feel a profound sense of vulnerability, knowing that my mother, our protector, was herself terrified.

It was her strength, her unwavering resolve to protect us, that gave us the glimmer of hope we clung to that night. I often think about what might have become of us if she hadn't been as resolute and determined as she was. She shielded us from the full force of the impending disaster, and I will be forever grateful for her unyielding courage. Even now, when hurricane season approaches, the memories of that night come rushing back, uninvited and unwelcome. I've never truly been able to overcome the deep-seated fear and anxiety it left in its wake. The emotions I experienced that night, the fear, the desperation, will forever be etched into my memory, just as it is in my mother's.

We were fortunate that my uncle lived in such close proximity to us, for without his nearness, I can't fathom how we would have found a safe haven that night. Although sleep eluded us, we felt safer in his apartment, away from the relentless fury of the storm. I can still picture families wading through waist-deep water outside, searching for higher ground. The hurricane's duration was unexpected; it lingered for hours, the rain relentless and unceasing. Even though we were on the second floor, the fear of flooding was an ever-present companion. That night was a harrowing journey through the depths of fear and despair, but it also revealed the strength and resilience that exists within us. It taught me the importance of community, the bonds of family, and the significance of coming together during times of adversity like the extreme weather all us of were experiencing. The scars of that night may never fully fade, but they serve as a constant reminder of the power of human endurance and the indomitable spirit that can arise even in the face of the most formidable challenges.

In the days following the flood, we returned to our apartment, only to find everything ruined. Unfortunately, we didn't have insurance to cover the damages, and my mom, a single mother to two children and an immigrant, was left to pick up the pieces on her own. Her job, which was in the food industry, couldn't reopen until the renovations were complete, and she couldn't afford to remain unemployed. So, we had to make a difficult decision and leave behind everything we knew, moving to Virginia to start anew. This personal experience has made me acutely aware of the inequalities in society when it comes to dealing with extreme weather events. It's a stark reminder that not everyone has the resources or support they need to recover from such disasters. It's a topic that needs more attention and action. Since that fateful day,

I've become acutely aware of the power and impact of weather on our lives. It's a phenomenon that should never be underestimated. The intricate interplay of various components that can dramatically change outcomes is nothing short of magical. While we lost much in the process, it has also ignited my passion for understanding and addressing the impacts of extreme weather and inequality it comes with in our world.

Inequality and Extreme Weather Events
by Joshua Mendoza

Extreme weather events like hurricanes in Southeast Texas can be devastating to the general population, however, while they affect every person in the area there is one populous in which these types of events can be a turn for the worse in quality of life and sustainability. Inequality in society is the lack of power and opportunities available for those born economically disadvantaged; inequality can also be about skin color giving the population of African Americans and Hispanics/Latinos in our region and over the United States significantly harder lives than white people. Thus the populous most affected by events like this is the older, poorer, and/or colored population. This brings the argument that extreme weather events and inequality in the Southeast Texas area go hand in hand and give the more fortunate and wealthy class an upper hand in preparing for, during, and after such catastrophic events due to economic and racial disadvantages.

Race and economic classes play a major part in every person's life whether they are wealthy or poor; and whether they are colored or white. Starting off with class; classes are often within the region of Southeast Texas and are often separated into 4 distinct categories the lower/impoverished class, the lower middle class, the higher middle class, and the upper/wealthy class. There are many races within the small section that is this region of Texas often including African Americans, Hispanics/Latinos, any people of Asian descent, and finally white people. Class and Race as seen in many places in America and especially here in Southeast Texas go hand in hand as the lower class and the lower middle class often consist of Black and Brown individuals due to race playing a major role in society as a whole; whereas the higher middle class and the wealthy class consist of a majority of white and people of Asian descent. These class distinctions are important as they give a clear indicator of what type of actions a person can take in events like hurricanes. Before a hurricane even happens there is often a period of time when people flock to grocery stores and buy up all of the supplies causing shortages and leaving many without food or water. Those in higher classes such as the upper class and the higher middle class are often some of the first to go buy out in large quantities and they can do so easily due to their race and the amount of accumulated wealth; this wealth allows them to stock up without worrying too much as to how it will affect them after the hurricane or any other major weather events are over. In comparison those with darker colored skin tones who reside in the lower classes such as the impoverished class and the lower middle class have to scrape for money and often are not able to afford or even get their hands on the supplies they need to make it through an event like this; These events often leave them starving or if they do spend money leave them in ruin afterward.

Though class plays a big factor before and after an extreme weather event several other problems arise while the actual storm or event plays out. These problems are often overlooked and not analyzed or worried about if the people are not immediate family; These people include the older population and the number of people with mental and/or mental incapacities/ disabilities. For the older population in the event of a tornado or similar storm, it is hard for this part of the populous to gather their things and leave the area that will be affected by the storm. They are often overlooked by many and if they are not part of a person's immediate family they are left behind and allowed to their own devices which often leads to them being in danger; This includes a number of situations such as sudden cardiac arrest due to stress, inability to walk for long periods of time, other major mobility issues, etc. Alongside the older adults, there are many people from children all the way into adulthood before becoming a part of the senior population who have mental or physical limitations that do not allow them to get to safety in a timely fashion. These impairments not only include any mental disabilities that a person was born with but also physical limitations such as missing limbs or paralyzation. A given example of this was the most recent hurricanes or tropical storms to hit the Southeast Texas area. This left many areas flooded and the water in some places reached even the rooftops of some buildings and houses. In events like these, what options are left to those individuals who were left behind in these two very big groups supposed to have? There is a very real possibility that these people could just perish due to the lack of help and the inability to be able to help themselves to the point of survival.

The aftermath of an extreme storm is often hard to look at and will undoubtedly take a long time to clean up and take care of afterward, but the most affected by this are often the lower classes rather than those in the higher classes. There are always so many destroyed properties, cars, and areas of land after a hurricane/ tropical storm. This is where class inequalities really play a massive role in the economic development of the area, and the pricing of materials and other necessary items for rebuilding. Those people in the lower classes as mentioned previously have very little to no money to begin with. They are often found for example in Beaumont in what people call the poorer areas which tends to be North and Northeast Beaumont along with other areas sprinkled throughout the city. These houses tend to be in lower levels of elevation and very close to the ground making it easier for water to pool up and destroy countless houses and apartment buildings. Whereas within the "Rich" neighborhoods as its called by the general population are often at a higher elevation in their yards and the houses themselves are now being built up even more by adding some more dirt to the area of the house foundations making it nearly impossible for these housing locations to be nearly as decimated as the housing in lower-income households and apartments. Situations like these only made the poor become more impoverished and in some cases not able to financially recover. Since materials for rebuilding would be in high demand and in low supply prices were bound to skyrocket and the only ones able to afford the necessary materials for rebuilding whatever got destroyed would be the wealthy. The economic shift caused by this might be temporary but when capitalized by businesses that undoubtedly are run by already wealthy people serves to line their own pockets causing an even bigger imbalance of power than before. This huge storm's aftermath does not affect the wealthy population nearly as much as others who genuinely need the money and are unable to amass enough wealth to move into a better area.

Inequalities and be found in many shapes and forms no matter where you go. However, this is very apparent when you travel to Southeast Texas; Despite the good economy found here in certain areas and businesses if someone truly opens their eyes to this area there is impoverishment and inequality everywhere. Most of this inequality is due to class distinctions which make it improbable and impossible to get into a higher class group than the person is already in. Also, though people like to believe race is not a huge factor in success when you look at the wealthy people in this area it tends to all look the same WHITE; though it is possible for any person to succeed as we see more and more African Americans and Hispanic/Latino people amass some wealth and success these are all outliers in a bigger more impoverished population. These are not the only inequalities found in the area either the senior and the incapacitated population also suffer from lack of resources and attention directed towards their problem. These unequal opportunities handed to the populations make it very simple to see the connection between extreme events like these without even getting into a debate about climate change. If a temporary effect like a storm on an area like Southeast Texas can have visible flaws and inequalities between people, there is no telling how much worse it could get in the future when the long-term effect of something like climate change settles in. We are living in a modern age where there should be less inequality but it is still ever present in the face of adversities such as storms and climate change.

Untitled

by Mason Miller

It was a Monday morning , and all I heard was a loud buzz from my room at seven in the morning but I'm the type of person to ignore so I turned it off. I had gone back to sleep because my school doesn't start until 8:30. Thirty minutes had past and the buzz kept getting louder and louder every minute when I was in a deep sleep. Then I finally woke up , but i was deciding if I wanted to go to school or not but this was the first year I was going to have perfect attendance so I was going to go no matter what. All I thought about in my head was my mom being proud of me because she works nights and does not see me In the morning. The first thing I do when I wake up is check my phone, and when I checked it all you see is 15 missed calls from my mother and my dad, 5 amber alerts, and a 2 message from my friend.

My jaw dropped to the floor and all I was thinking about is what happened. A few minutes later I got up to get out of my bed because I was running late and I had to get to school on time no matter what's the cost. It was pretty dark in my room , but there was a strange sound outside and a wet feeling on my feet, I didn't mind it tho because my little brother always make noise and spill things everywhere. So I continued to get dressed in the dark , then when I got done getting dressed my mother called me AGAIN. So I answered then she sounded relieved and said "son there's an extreme flood warning" and she told me I had the choice to go to school or not. She told me not to go because it was an amber alert and she was worried but I told her I'm going to school no matter what mom. She then said ok son be careful.

When I was done being on the phone with my mom I grabbed my water bottle then headed out to the bus stop. But there was something odd. First I went to check my brother's room because I continued to feel a wet feeling and kept hearing loud noises, But they were all sleep. I tried turning on my light but it wouldn't work. The loud noises got louder and the wet feeling grew to my ankles but the noises sounded like it was from the outside. I headed to the door and a gust of wind and rain hit me while there's one big dark cloud and thundering noises.

I was in so much shock I called my mom back and said mom there's a flood and a huge thunderstorm. How are you going to get home to us? I said in my frightened voice. She told me it's going to be fine. I'll be there soon. I woke my brothers up and said pack your things that's not on top of shelves so it doesn't get flooded. I called my dad back he asked me was I fine I told him not really, at that moment I did not know what to do I had my brothers to take care of and I was scared on how bad the flood was going to get. I asked my dad how are you and my mom going to get home to us while the flood is here. My dad stated well find a way don't worry. I checked the message my friend sent me it said "Hey bro I hope your doing ok during this flood don't be scared well get through it.

After thirty minutes the thunder got louder and I heard a boom near my neighborhood. It came from east of me and that's exactly where my friend. . . . I prayed to god that it did not hit my friends house. Me and my brothers were in the living room where everything was packed at sitting there waiting for my parents in the dark. The room was filled with two feet of water. so as timed by pass I had got a little of connection and my mother called me and when i picked up she told me to come outside so we can go to the emergency center that's where helicopters were picking people up and moving them somewhere safe with their belongings. I asked my mom where is her car she said it's gone she will tell me about it later. My dad was finding a way we could get to the emergency center without walking but we continued to walk till we got closer then we spotted my dad on the boat with people while the water was three feet tall at that moment. we had to yell and wave then seconds later we caught his attention. He pointed over there then the boat came to us.

An hour later we was at the emergency center thanking god that we made it out alive. That was the craziest experience I've ever had because I had to take care of my brothers and all of that. Good thing we are in a safe place now.

The Sun Does Not Always Symbolize Happiness
by Ilahi Modh

When someone thinks of Inequality, the first thing that may come to mind is gender, social, or racial inequality. What may not be realized is that this is just the tip of the iceberg. One form of inequality that is completely overlooked is inequality dealing with extreme weather. Extreme weather ranges from extreme cold to extreme heat and torrential snow to torrential rain. Texas is no exception to experiencing extreme weather. By far Texas may have the most variety of extreme weather in the United States, from hurricanes to snow storms and even recently, extreme heat. During this summer, Texas faced record-breaking heat levels. Although many may have thought little of it since they had the privilege of having air conditioning and a roof over their heads, the heat was not this easy to beat for everyone. For one man, Franklin, he experienced the worst side of inequality, which eventually sparked the idea of change.

This scorching summer was relentless. Temperatures soared to record highs. This heat created a divide between those who could seek shelter from the blistering sun and those who had to tolerate its ruthless heat. Among the countless victims of this weather inequality was a homeless man named Franklin. Franklin was a tough man with a heart of resilience. He had been living on the streets for years. He had found comfort in the underbelly of the city. Under a bridge that provided some meager shade was the place he called home. However, this summer was unlike any other and his cover under the bridge was not sufficient enough. The heatwave was relentless, and finding a break from the heat became a life-or-death challenge for Franklin and many like him. As the city baked under the blistering sun, Franklin went from being at ease every day under the bridge to having his daily routine become a punishing battle for survival. His usual sources of relief, like public libraries and cooling centers, were overcrowded, making it difficult for him to find refuge. The heat was a constant foe. It made Franklin's worn-out clothes cling to his sweaty body. One scorching afternoon, Franklin hit his limit. Franklin's health took a turn for the worse. Dehydration and heatstroke threatened his life. With a blade of luck, a passerby, Maria, noticed Franklin's distress and rushed to his aid. She called for an ambulance and stayed by his side until help arrived. Franklin's life was saved, but this was not near the end of Franklin's story. This incident shed light on the harsh reality of weather inequality. Franklin's story gained traction from local activists and organizations working to address homelessness and extreme weather conditions. It sparked a citywide conversation about the need for better support systems during heatwaves for the homeless and everyone in vulnerable situations. Soon after, programs were expanded, providing water stations, cooling shelters, and medical services for those without homes and others who needed these services. The city came to the realization that no one deserves this kind of inequality, especially in circumstances where it is life-threatening.

In conclusion, Franklin's near-death experience started a great change in the city. The city took a step towards weather equality, recognizing that extreme weather events could affect anyone, regardless of their housing situation. Franklin's strength and Maria's kindness started a shift in the way the city approached extreme heat, making it a more bearable season for everyone, especially those like Franklin who had once been forgotten. Although this story is fictional, it gives insight into the lives of the people affected and what we can do as a community to aid these people. After all, everybody deserves equality.

Mother Nature's Wrath
by Camren Nichols

The TV plays loudly in the background as my parents move quickly throughout the house grabbing clothes, and lifting furniture, and my dad places sandbags outside our doors. My little sister and I sit on the ground and play Go Fish to pass the time, but I can't help but listen to the TV occasionally. The weatherman is talking about some hurricane coming in from the gulf that is about to hit. I honestly don't even know why my parents are so worried, our house has never flooded before, even during Ike.

"Do you have any sevens?" My sister asks to which I nod slowly before handing over my seven hearts. I'm somehow losing to a seven-year-old whose favorite card to ask for is sevens. I should know by now what she wants yet I'm too distracted by the chaos that is sweeping through my house.

I lean back from where I sit to see my mom and dad whispering to each other in the kitchen. Dad runs his hands through his hair as he attempts to comfort my mom as she aggressively whispers about damage to our home.

I move back to my original position and ask, "Do you have any . . . sevens?" My sister frowns before handing me a card, so I celebrate loudly just to rub it in her face. She knocks the cards out of my hand before sticking her tongue at me leaving me no other option but to nudge her face out of mine.

"Hey! Stop fighting and pick those cards up." My dad nags as he passes through the living room to head back outside. Dark, almost black clouds form in the distance, which look vastly different from the occasional rain we've been getting on and off today.

My sister and I slowly pick up the cards, but not without the occasional insults thrown at each other with smiles on our faces. "It'll come in from the gulf then hit in places like Corpus Christi before continuing to move up," the tiny man from Channel 6 says as he drags his hand up from the Gulf of Mexico and brings it up towards Texas.

I look out the window and see water rushing down the street as it begins to storm. "Do you think our house will flood?" My sister says absentmindedly as she closes the card box. "No. No, the house will be fine," I say sitting closer to her and putting an arm around her, "Dad said the house has never flooded, even during Ike." She nods and then stands to put up the cards. I look outside once more and see a branch fall off a tree from across the street.

That night my sister and I share my bed because according to my mom, we should stick together for now. My sister snoozes away blissfully beside me while I stay up listening to the crack of thunder every few minutes. I can tell my mom and dad are still up because of the light that slips through the sliver under my door. Plus their voices carry through the wood every once in a while before quieting back down.

"John, we need to leave at some point. There's no waiting this one out." My mom says exasperated. They quiet down again, but I get out of bed, hoping to hear what's said. I don't want to leave our home. What if something bad happens to it?

"We'll leave if necessary, but you know we don't have the money to just leave on a whim," I hear Dad agree before the scrape of the chairs signifies the end of the conversation.

I hurriedly rush back to the safety of my bed to not get caught still being up just as they open the door to check on us. I keep my eyes sealed shut, hoping to trick them into thinking I'm asleep. They kiss our heads before leaving the room, likely to go to bed themselves. I stare up at the ceiling as the roar of the storm continues and begin counting sheep in an attempt to fall asleep.

"Syd, wake up. Come on, let's get up," I hear a voice say as I'm slowly woken up from my sleepy daze. I pry my eyes open to see mom holding my little sister who has tears streaking down her face. I look over in time to see my dad frantically pass my door as he runs to the front of the house. "Come on sweetie. Grab some shoes, we're about to leave," My mom rubs my arms trying to wake me up some more. I look down at the floor and see our carpet is beginning to be soaked with water.

"Mom, what's going on?" I throw my blankets off and tiptoe on the ground to my closet. I shove my feet into tennis shoes as my mom says, "The water rose a lot quicker than we thought, we're getting water in the house." She places down my sister whose tears have dried up and stands silently in the middle of the room. She grabs an overnight bag from the top of my closet before tossing in pairs of shirts and pants. "Where are we gonna go?" I ask, tears beginning to fill my eyes. My mom stops what she's doing to cradle my face in her hands, kissing the tip of my nose, and says, "Don't worry sweetheart. Your dad and I have something planned out." She gives me a smile before continuing what she was doing.

"Y'all almost ready to go? We need to hurry." My dad pokes his head into my room with two bags thrown over his shoulder. My mom quickly picks up my bag then makes me grab my little sister's hand. We walk to our front door where two guys in yellow rain jackets are grabbing our bags and yelling something to another guy in a boat where our street was just a few hours ago. My mouth falls open as I see how far the water has gone up our yard.

"I need y'all to be my brave little girls, okay?" My dad says, crouching in front of me and my sister and rubbing the tops of our heads. We both slowly nod before one of the yellow jacket guys carries off my sister into the growing depth of water in our front yard and then the other lifts me off my feet.

As we trudge through the water I can't help but look back at our home and just hope we can be back soon. Once we're all loaded up, I can no longer tell if the wetness on my face is from the rain that seeps through my jacket and into my clothes or tears as I leave my home to face the wrath of Mother Nature.

Untitled
by Gabrielle Owens

Many people go through difficulties during hurricane season especially in Southeast Texas. I have witnessed this first hand when I was helping the poorer class in Port Arthur at the airport get off the helicopters they had just evacuated their homes from. Have you ever thought about the inequality these people have to go through?

During Hurricane Harvey, I went to the airport located at the edge of Beaumont. I helped people get off of helicopters and bring them to get fresh clothes. Most of the people had to leave all of their belongings and were soaked in dirty sewage water from the hurricane when their houses got flooded. This was eye opening for me because I saw how sad and lost these people looked. Many of these people lost their cars and no longer had a way of transportation. Something as simple as a car can mean a lot to someone. Cars are expensive and many people have to work for them and may not have the best car insurance because of what is able to fit into their budget. Many people also were worried about what they were going to do for work at this time and expressed it in multiple ways since many of their places of work had been flooded.

When the hurricane hit, it showed me that not many people have places to go when extreme weather devastations happen. They were stuck at the airport with clothing that wasn't theirs and had to change in public areas. They also were not able to receive proper food at this time. We could only provide snacks at the airport because there was not a place for people to be able to cook. The people that came to the airport had been dehydrated and not nourished for hours. This made me feel like we weren't equal because I knew when I was done volunteering I was going to be able to go home and receive proper food and clean water. I also knew I had a way to get back home and a house that was still on the ground. This taught me to be more thankful for the things I have and not take them for granted.

To conclude, extreme weather shows true inequality in our society. Everyone does not have the same opportunities to bounce back from hurricanes. Many people also have to work harder than others to regain what they lost.

Extreme Weather and Inequality
by Parth Patel

Katrina a girl in a fit of rage,
A storm in the year of two-thousand five.
In a city diverse as New Orleans,
A city filled with many different types of people;
A city filled with rich and poor
A city filled with many races and much diversity.
The rich fled as far as money would allow them,
The poor could not go anywhere.
The poor stayed despite knowing of Katrina's rage.
Not only did Katrina break homes
She flooded the city,
All in a fit of rage.
In a time racism was rampant,
Katrina only hurt the poor.
The poor were black
And America tried to turn her back,
But the people retaliated
Using words as weapons,
People began to ask what if . . .
What if the victims were rich
What if the victims weren't black
Would America still turn her back?

Thunder and Storms
by Kennedy Perkins

In the storm of life, we stand,
Witnessing the great divide on this land.
The sky roars with anger, unleashing fears,
As humans battle inequity that churns over the years.

From polar vortex to hurricane's rage,
Socioeconomic gaps, an unfair stage.
Communities separated by a widening rift,
When nature's wrath thrusts, all set adrift.

The wealthy find shelter behind their walls,
The poor are left scrambling as disaster befalls.
Unequal are we in the face of the storm,
As the earth's fury takes on its cruelest form.

Extreme weather is no longer rare,
Yet still, some deny its existence and glare.
Through drought, wildfire, and relentless floods,
The global disparity quietly thuds.

But in these dark moments where divisions loom,
A ray of hope pierces desperation and gloom.
Hand in hand, a resilient force takes stride,
An army to challenge injustice and provide.

For when humanity unites with compassion,
Nature's own fury shall never dampen.
Believe in the power to balance the scales—
That our collective spirit in unity prevails.

Untitled
by baile randle

They had extreme weather In New Orleans and inequality in 2005. A lot of things were unfair for blacks. It took basically years for them to get their houses and lives together. The horror show at the Superdome close to 25,000 people were trapped there for days in the blazing sun stink. They had no food or water because of that more than 1800 people died out there.

Ray Nagin was the one to say something about the crisis on the radio. It was literally a history of extreme weather. People that were healthy didn't care.

Almost 80% of New Orleans was flooded. Billions and gallons of water was covering up the city. The flood walls even broke. People would say Katrina was an equal storm no matter what race. It wasn't though, you would more than 5x pf people who lost their home in the flooding because they were african american and not a white homeowner. The recovery was also not an equal opportunity. White neighborhoods after Katrina looked back nice after they could actually fix it up. African americans had to or wanted to wait for the government but were still getting no access to building back their homes.

The government didn't even show up when everyone was stranded for 5 days at the Superdome. In New Orleans they danced and sang happy or sad; it didn't matter. Only 37% of its pre Katrina residents have returned. Thousands were still destroyed even though charities have fixed hundreds of homes.

Someone else's roof was on top of a lady named Betty Bell's house. She was finally allowed back for a look a month after Katrina demolished it. She owned a black business, and her insurance settlement was nowhere nearly enough to rebuild. It took 10 years to finally start rebuilding because she was african american. For many Katrina victims it ended up a bureaucratic nightmare. African American neighborhoods were significantly lower than similar homes in white neighborhoods.

Hurricane Katrina is the coldest to ever hit the United states. Lets not forget about the animals. People have attachments to their pets. I have attachment every time my dog dies. I get sad literally every time so just imagine in a pandemic. I would be stressed about things plus I love and have earned are all gone. It's like my life would be falling apart. There's nothing they can do about their animals dying during the pandemic. They're trying to save themselves first and their children and families.

Us as people of color don't deserve the way we get treated. Whites should want to help or just people with color should come together to help each other. As I wrote the government wasn't really worried about all those people staying at the Superdome all that time so, why would he care to help them get back on their feet. Stick together through thick or thin like brothers and sisters and us people will make it out.

Ancient to the Future Project
by Brady Redding

Since the dawn of human civilization, we have made innovations and transformed our environment to make life easier for ourselves. As time has passed, however, with the development of society and the division into classes, progress has been endlessly stalled by large corporations. This reality is clearly encapsulated in our current predicament that is the threat of the extreme weather that results from climate change and our inaction on it.

Currently, we have already reached a point in which irreversible damage has been done. This can clearly be seen this past summer, with it being the hottest summer on record in human history. Even if one is not familiar with the science behind global warming, it can easily be noticed that it has been much hotter than it used to be. This extreme heat is also paralleled by extreme cold. This can be seen when, in 2021, major winter storms hit the United States. In Texas, this issue was exacerbated by the failure of the power grid, leaving millions without power. In the end, this crisis resulted in over preventable 200 deaths. Due to Texas' power grid being privately owned by several companies, they are more focused on making the most money while incurring the lowest possible expenses. As a result, the Texas power grid was not properly prepared for an event such as this, due to the fact that it would cost extra money to do so. This issue luckily did not come into play in Beaumont, as we are on Louisiana's power grid. However, for me personally, I did come into contact with this issue when it occurred. At the time, I was in Pflugerville, Texas, staying with my father, and while we did not lose electricity, there were people in our area that did. Events like this caused by extreme weather will only continue to occur if greenhouse gas emissions are not lowered.

The largest contributor to greenhouse gas emissions is the fossil fuel industry. Due to our reliance on fossil fuels, this industry is massively profitable. As a result, they have gained unimaginable wealth and power. As such, given the fact that moving towards clean energy alternatives would hurt their business, they have done everything in their power to control the narrative and to obstruct any legislation that would restrict the fossil fuel industry. A great example of this is ExxonMobil. In the 1970s, ExxonMobil's climate scientists had determined that the actions of the fossil fuel industry were raising the planet's temperature. Rather than take action to prevent this, ExxonMobil hid this information from the public and started to fund propaganda with the intent to mislead and lie about global warming, climate change, and their direct contribution to them. Despite the obvious lack of morality, given their position, this was a very logical decision. Rather than lose out on their current guaranteed profits, they could just ignore the problem and continue to make billions. At climate conferences scientists often speak of returns on investment in clean energy initiatives, but why would any corporation pursue that venture when they can simply continue what they are doing without having to wait for a return on their investment? This exposes that this problem is more related to our economic system than one might think.

In today's world, in the United States, wealth is so concentrated at the top that the richest 1% of Americans are worth around the same amount as the bottom 90% of Americans. Consequently, these people have much more power to influence the policies of this country. They do this through corporate lobbying, which is essentially just legalized bribery. This allows the rich to prevent the passage of any legislation that goes against their material interest, such as increasing the minimum wage, increasing the corporate tax rate, or, most relevant to this situation, regulation of industry. This practice is a big part of why our politics here in the United States are so biased in favor of corporations. Even those who come into politics with good intentions often become corrupt after seeing how much money that they can receive by being corporate dogs. A great recent example of this is Kyrsten Sinema, a once progressive minded individual who is now best known for obstructing the passage of policy in the U.S. Senate that she previously supported, like increasing the federal minimum wage. As such, this direct corruption of officials has facilitated the death of American democracy. The wealthy use the power that their accumulated capital gives them to maintain a status quo in which society runs for their benefit, no matter how many people are negatively impacted by it. This has served as a major roadblock to fighting climate change, as, while it helps, individual actions will not be enough. A federal plan is needed to facilitate the massive changes that will need to take place across the country in infrastructure. With this in mind, the wealthiest Americans must find ways to justify their position, as if they were to reveal the truth, the American public would immediately turn against them. Therefore, they mislead the public with concepts that no longer exist in the United States, like meritocracy.

The wealthy in the United States often try to defend their position as being one that was awarded to them solely through hard work, or intelligence, however, that is very often not the case. For instance, a common perpetrator of this act and also one of the richest people on Earth, Elon Musk, tries to portray himself as a workaholic that made it to the top through hard work and dedication. However, in reality, Musk came from a wealthy family that benefited from apartheid in South Africa. This can also be seen with Jeff Bezos, who received hundreds of thousands of dollars from his family to start Amazon. Furthermore, Musk and Bezos have both received billions of dollars from the government for their companies. In fact, Musk's company, Tesla, would probably no longer exist if not for the $465 million dollar low interest loan that it received from the government in 2010. The fact that, despite this information being publicly available, he still pretends to be "self-made" is incredibly insulting to those who work hard every day to make the same amount of money in a year as he makes in the blink of an eye. The average worker works infinitely harder than and deals with infinitely more stress than Musk, who at any point in time, could stop working and relax for the rest of his life, yet due to his narcissism he feels the need to stroke his own ego and as such has built a cult of personality comprising of misguided individuals on the internet.

With these things in mind, the problem of climate change cannot be combatted without first combating inequality. We need to take back control of our government from the wealthy, who are in direct opposition to us in their material interests. We should not be giving these already extremely rich corporations money to do what they should be doing anyway. We should be throwing these executives in jail for intentionally destroying the planet. We should be rebuilding America's infrastructure to be based upon green energy alternatives. We should be uplifting impoverished communities. We should be eliminating homelessness. These are just some examples, but much more should be included on this list. None of these things are impossible. As the richest country on Earth, we are capable of these things. It is simply that we are not organized enough right now to do so.

Therefore, while we have already reached a point in which we will face some of the consequences of climate change, that does not mean we should give up. We may be against some of the wealthiest people in the world, but we have a numbers advantage. As a wise man once said, "There are decades where nothing happens; and there are weeks where decades happen."

Drowning
by Arismel Reyes

Carmen

The day my family and I went under water was the day I went under within myself. The worst flood my town has experienced seemed to last for weeks. My mother, father, two brothers, and myself had to be rescued by a boat since we could no longer find our home liveable. I felt helpless and useless. I kept wondering "why us?", and I'm guessing my mother saw the worriedness in my face since she kept repeating "it's OK mija" into my ear. All I could do was look outward to the big houses, "man son" as my pa likes to call them, and thought how things would be different if we had been blessed with great wealth.

Ezra

The town is hit with such a major flood. I've watched from the third floor the boats passing by with families in them as they drove them to safety. On one, I witnessed the face of one of the most worried kids I've ever seen. She seemed to be around my age, and I wondered where they're going. My father has informed us to pack our bags because the helicopter is ready. I wonder where we're going. I hope somewhere there's a beach because I want to swim, but not in this flood water.

Carmen

The man from the boat took us to a place far from our home full of infected water. This place looked like a shelter and inside were people who were rescued just like us. I wonder how they felt having to leave everything behind. They gave us blankets and sandwiches of either ham or turkey when we arrived, which was nice since I haven't eaten anything the whole day. They announced that we will have to stay here for at least a week or until the water went down some. At night, we slept in three beds, one for my mom and I, another for my two brothers, and the last one went to my dad. We woke up, ate breakfast, met new people, ate lunch, talked some more, ate dinner, worried about the after, went back to sleep, and repeated. This was my life for a week if not longer. I felt that I was growing paranoid being stuck here with nothing but my thoughts about how we'll be able to survive going back home.

Ezra

We arrived at what I'm guessing would be Chicago. The beautiful non-water infected windy city. After checking into the hotel that mother chose, we went into the diner to get something to eat. I could really go for a hamburger right about now. After dinner I decided to just stay in for the night. In the morning, I woke up, got dressed, went out to see some new places I've seen online. Throughout the day, I've tried some of the best food I've tasted. When I got back to the hotel, my parents were talking about what should be done to the house when we get back home. Father said we should hire professionals to clean the house while we wait out here, but my mothers had the idea of never going back and just staying out here. To me, it didn't matter what they chose to do after our town went back to normal. I went back to my room and went to sleep. When I woke up, I couldn't decide what to do for the day due to the infinite choices this city had to offer.

Carmen

The flood finally died down and we were allowed to go back home. My heart was filled with excitement and horror at the same time. I don't know if I could handle the sight of our now probably destroyed home. When a rescue car dropped us off at the front of our house, I swear I almost fainted. The house, no longer our home, was marked with a black line all around indicating how high the water got. Everything inside was trashed onto the floor and dirty from the water. I'm scared. What's going to happen to us now? I don't know how we're going to recover from this with just the income of our parents, which just to say, is not a lot. It'll take us a while to get the house clean, paint it, replace anything broken, check household machines, and other things I can't think of right now. The only thought on my mind is "I can't believe it."

Ezra

We arrived back to our town once father said the water was gone, which was a bummer since I was having fun exploring the grounds of Chicago. We saw the house and the damage that was very apparent. The black line surrounding the house was turning green from the infected water. Fortunately, only the first floor was hit so it won't be too much of a bother to get it redone. After all this, I can't wait to go back to how things were, but unfortunately, I'll have to wait a few weeks for that to happen. This would be the most boring time of my life.

Carmen

"This is going to be the hardest time of our lives."

Ezra

"This is going to be the boring-est time of my life."

Lake of Memories
by Reagan Rigby

Events can take over your life like a storm can sink a ship. It's all quiet in the moment, but in a flash, in the blink of an eye, with the snap of a finger to the palm, it's gone. Everything you earned. Every memory. Every piece of trash that would cause you to constantly complain to your kids about chores. Every piece of dignity. Gone.

Attempting to conceal her panic, Michelle Rigby hurriedly scooped up her infant son and rocked him in her arms while they solemnly watched the news broadcast. After the reporters revealed the heart shattering news that the crest level had risen to a minimum of 28 feet, with a sense of purpose she was immediately off to snatch heartfelt things she knew they'd need to save. With her breaths intensifying by every second, she grabbed the enormous Santa bag that was in a corner at the top of her closet that they had used the previous Christmas—before she could find the will to begin stuffing her family's belongings inside of it, she took a moment to stare at it. No more than eight months ago they used this bag on one of the happiest days of the year, and here she was now using it as a way to save years of memories.

Corey was walking through the sun room when he heard quick footsteps making their way towards him from the living room. He saw Michelle emerge from behind the wall holding their infant with lines of worry creased on her face that his heart dropped to the bottom of his stomach. "Baby please look at this," Michelle grabbed his arm and pulled him towards the living room so that he could see the T.V. There they stood on their floral carpet that ended at the kitchen that had unfortunately come with the house, thinking about how their white-picket neighborhood they had always loved was about to turn into a lake of memories.

They prepared for the hell that was to come as best they could by setting important things at least four feet high, and had already bought supplies they knew they would need like food, water, diapers and anything else that would help them handle being flooded in for a couple weeks. Later that evening, the soul shattering news was announced—the crest projection had jumped to 30 feet, and in a panic Michelle and Corey moved them and their son to their bedroom above the garage so that their baby wouldn't wake up with water in his bed. Clinging to each other to find comfort and hope, Shelley and Corey held their infant between them like a sandwich as they watched the crest rise to 34 feet on their phones.

Around 2:30 am, still awake with bags forming under her eyes, Michelle walked downstairs to snatch a few of her son's things that she knew he would want if they had to evacuate. She dreadfully opened the door to the house to find that the water had got to six inches. Slowly making her way to Jacob's room, she felt the floorboards beneath her shifting as she carefully navigated the house. She felt her belly kick, and quietly assured the life in her stomach that she'd be careful to not lose her footing. She made sure to grab her son's favorite set of toys—the transformers that his room had been themed in since he was a newborn.

BANG *BANG* *BANG* is what woke Shelley and Corey at four in the morning. It was the loudest bangs they had ever heard, so frightened and worried their baby would wake up, Shelley hurried downstairs—what she opened the door to find was earth shattering—their garage fridges and freezers were floating and banging into each other, creating small cracks in the rolls. The water now reached the landing on the stairway heading upstairs and was about two feet deep. "Wow," she heard a shocked voice behind her, and turning around to look at her husband's face, a tear slowly dripped down his face and into the pool below them. "What do we do? Do we leave? Do we wake up the baby? What do we do?" Corey's voice was becoming more broken with every word he spoke.

"What we do is wait," Shelley took his hand and held it to her heart. Corey looked at her with the most worried face she had ever seen. "The baby is still sleeping and we need to let him. We also have to think about the one in here," Shelley pointed to her stomach. "I don't want to stress her out too much."

"No, no I know, you're right," Corey said in a shaky breath. "Let's aim for daylight. That'll give the baby enough time to sleep."

In agreement the two walked back upstairs and admired Jacob as he slept for the next hour and a half.

Five-thirty in the morning is when they heard the ring of a phone call. Corey and Shelley looked at each other for a moment, and Corey slowly picked up his cell to answer. "My friends rode out the storm. All they have left is a boat and are getting as many people out as possible. If y'all want to get out, now is the time, Corey" is what Shelley heard on the other line. The time between that call and the knock on the door telling them the boat was ready was filled with pure tension. It was them wondering if they would ever get to see their house again, worried about the baby forming life in Shelley's stomach, worried that this experience would cause trauma to their two year old son.

Hearing that knock on the door was like hearing the angel's trumpets. After grabbing what they could as fast as possible, it was time they woke up their son from his peaceful slumber, probably dreaming about transformers. "Hey, Bubba," Shelley whispered as she moved that one curly lock that hung lower than the rest of Jacob's hair. "We have to go for a boat ride."

It was the wave of a tsunami when they opened the door to leave. "Hey buddy, is this your first boat ride?" asked one of the young men who had come to rescue them. Jacob's confident "Yup," made Shelley's heart skip a beat. Knowing their little man wasn't scared made everything that much easier—she knew they were ready. She wrapped him in a quilt and coat she had grabbed before they left, and Corey carried him outside into thigh-high water. As soon as they stepped out, their boots immediately filled with water, and trying to walk through the current made them feel like cats trying to pull a sleigh through snow. The wooshes of the wind overtook Shelley's ears and the raindrops on her glasses made it difficult for her to see anything else. Once on the boat, the rescuers sprayed a large yellow circle on their garage door letting any rescuers know their house was empty. Through the foggy and rain smeared glasses, Shelley could see all of the lights from their house reflecting off the water creating a beautiful glow.

When they took off, all they could feel was a bunch of tiny needles poking them. The rain was coming at them sideways and Jacob's parents were trying their best to shield him from it and keep him from feeling the jolts of the boat hitting mailboxes that were invisible in the dark water. As they escaped what was left of their neighborhood, they rode past a truck with its lights and windshield wipers on, obviously abandoned. Shelley could feel Jacob shivering from the harsh winds and rain, but when she looked down at him, he still seemed perfectly happy with this adventure that had pulled him out of his sleep. Within five minutes that felt like five years, they were on land and were able to climb up the hill to get to their truck.

The next few days were filled with waiting. The water would not recede and the neighborhood became an island, no one coming or going. When Corey returned a few days later, he was greeted with a "meow," from their very hungry cat and with seeing their years of memories and belongings in piles several feet high at the edge of the street.

The blessing of friends and family is what got them through this traumatic experience. Church groups from other states pulled all of the drywall and insulation out. Contacts through her husband's work showed up with tractors to haul everything to the road. A completely helpless situation became an inspiration to them. Seeing everyone pull together and work as a team was overwhelming.

Strangers, friends, family and neighbors were all volunteering their time and supplies to help everyone through their struggles, and they thank God everyday for the blessings they have received.

Interstellar Justice Seeker
by Armajah Robinson

Stellasia lived in a universe that was almost too perfect. The sun always shone, the birds always sang, and everyone was always happy. It was the kind of place where you could walk down the street and see a unicorn grazing on the lawn.

But there was a dark side to Stellasia's world. The scientists had discovered that it was too ideal. The scientists had also discovered that there were infinite parallel universes, each one with its own unique set of laws and possibilities. In some universes, the dinosaurs never went extinct. In others, humanity had colonized the stars. And in still others, magic was real. And all of these universes averaged out to what could be called True Reality. Universes closer to the True Reality would stay in existence for billions of years, but ones more strange and wild would risk popping out of existence if the choices of the people of that universe strayed too far from the behavior of the people of True Reality, the average of all universes. The difference in the level of existence closer to the center of all universes, the True Reality, and barely existing on the edge, was like the difference between rocks and clouds. Stellasia's universe was so far from the average reality that it was on the verge of not existing at all. So they decided to call their universe the Whisper Universe, because their world compared to other parallel worlds is just like a ghost or a breeze, only existing in the hopes and dreams of other, more real, universes.

In an effort to understand why their world was so dangerously on the edge of existence and nonexistence, the scientists had developed small ships called universe hoppers, which allowed them to travel between these parallel universes. They used the universe hopper to study different realities and to learn more about their own universe.

Stellasia was a curious and adventurous young girl. She had always dreamed of exploring the parallel universes, but she knew that it was forbidden. The scientists had warned her that it was too dangerous.

But Stellasia couldn't resist the temptation. One day, she stole a universe hopper and set off on her own adventure.

Stellasia traveled to many different universes. She saw things that she never imagined possible. She met aliens, robots, and even dragons. But she also saw universes that were much darker and more dangerous than her own.

One day, low on fuel, Stellasia accidentally found herself in the forbidden zone of the multiverse, called the Average Universe. The Average Universe was the closest universe to True Reality, and it was forbidden for anyone from the edge of reality, such as Stellasia's world, to visit this central zone. The Average Universe was considered sacred and taboo.

But as she slowly drifted through the clouds low on fuel, Stellasia's curiosity soon turned to shock, as this Average Universe was nothing like what she imagined. It was smelly and dirty. There was a thing called night. But she couldn't stay up in the air for hours, her tiny ship had to come down soon. For some reason, maybe from being too overwhelmed with the reality of what she saw, or maybe from her long journey, she began to feel sleepy, and fell asleep while piloting this ship.

Stellasia's universe hopper crashed into the backyard of a small, dilapidated house in the Average Universe. She emerged from the wreckage, dazed and confused. She looked around and saw that she was in a poor neighborhood. The streets were lined with trash and there were few trees to provide shade. The air was thick with pollution and the heat was unbearable.

Stellasia heard a noise coming from the house. She walked over to the door and knocked. A moment later, the door opened and a young girl appeared.

"Can I help you?" the girl asked. She seems more worried about what was in her house than the fact that a spaceship-time-machine combo had just crashed into her backyard.

"My name is Stellasia," Stellasia said. "I'm lost. Can you help me?"

The girl nodded. "Come in," she said. She didn't seem surprised at all. Maybe she watched a lot of science fiction movies, so she was prepared for this possibility, however unlikely.

Stellasia followed the girl into the house. It was small and cramped, but it was clean and tidy.

"My name is Novali," the girl said. "My dad is home sick, he's been like that for a month, so I'm skipping school to take care of him and my little brother while my mom is out working."

"I'm sorry to hear that," Stellasia said. "What's wrong with him?"

"He works in the factory," Novali said. "He gets sick a lot from the heat and the pollution."

Stellasia was shocked. She couldn't believe that people in this universe had to live in such unhealthy conditions.

"In my universe," she said, "the city cares enough to add trees to the sidewalks. They help catch pollution and provide shade. That way, people don't get sick so easily."

Novali's eyes widened. "Really?" she asked. "That sounds amazing." What Novali didn't want to mention was that the city did add beautiful, thick-leaved trees above sidewalks, but only on the nicer side of town where the tourists and business folk would stroll from their highrise jobs to their nearby coffee shop. Her side of town didn't get that sort of treatment.

Stellasia nodded. "It is," she said. "But I guess every universe has its own problems."

Novali smiled sadly. "Yes, it does," she said.

Stellasia and Novali talked for a long time that day. They talked about their families, their friends, and their dreams. Stellasia learned a lot about the challenges that people face in the Average Universe. And Novali learned a lot about the wonders of Stellasia's universe.

After a few weeks of living with Novali's family, Stellasia finally repaired her universe hopper. She promised Novali to return one day, but said she had to run, because the scientist from her Whisper Universe might find her if she sticks around in one world too long.

Six years later, Stellasia returned to the Normal Universe to check on Novali, but she was careful to stay in the shadows. She was still on the run after stealing the universe hopper, and she didn't want to risk getting caught. She decided to stay just a few weeks once she located her friend.

Stellasia found Novali living in a shelter with her younger sibling. Their home had been destroyed by a hurricane, and their school had been flooded. She was shocked to learn that Novali's father had died from a preventable illness. He had been unable to get the proper health care he needed due to being low income, and her mother was in jail after being caught stealing food at the gas station to feed her family. It was too much for Stellasia to process; it had been just a few years since she last visited. She had seen many parallel worlds, so she knew just how easy these tragedies could have been avoided.

Stellasia's heart broke for her friend. She wanted to help, but she knew that she was limited. She didn't have access to the resources of her own universe, and she couldn't stay in the Normal Universe for long without being discovered.

Stellasia watched as Novali struggled to survive. She saw her working long hours at a low-wage job, and she saw her struggling to help her younger sibling with their schoolwork, which was now all online, because her community lacked the funds to rebuild the school quickly. Stellasia also saw the toll that inequality was taking on Novali's health and well-being. Novali's hair was thinning, and her face looked grim.

One day, Stellasia overheard Novali somberly talking to her younger sibling.

"I wish we lived in a more just world," Novali said. "I wish everyone had access to the same opportunities, no matter the color of their skin or the money in their pocket."

Stellasia nodded in agreement. She knew that Novali was right. But she also knew that it would take a lot of hard work and dedication to create a more just world.

Stellasia made a decision. She would use her experiences in the Normal Universe to inspire other Universes to fight for change. Even though she couldn't save Novali, she would tell others the story of Novali and her struggles. She would show them the impact of inequality on people's lives. And she would encourage them to stand up for what is right. Stellasia knew that she couldn't change the world overnight. But she was determined to make a difference. She wanted to create a world where everyone had the same chance to succeed. Maybe, just maybe, she could shift True Reality to be closer to her perfect home world, and maybe the Whisper Universe would not be just as hope or a dream.

Togetherness
by Lexcey Savoy

In a world where storms rage and winds howl,
Inequality, too, rears its ugly scowl.
But hear me now, for I have a tale too,
Of the fight against both, where we all must dwell.

Extreme weather, a force so fierce and wild,
Affects us all, regardless of our style.
From hurricanes to droughts, nature's wrath unfurls,
Leaving devastation in its relentless swirls.

But let us not forget the other foe at hand,
Inequality, dividing our precious land.
For while the storm may pass, leaving scars behind,
Injustice lingers, a constant, cruel grind.

For some, the storms bring just minor delay,
While others lose everything, day by day.
The rich find refuge, their resources secure,
While the poor suffer, left without a cure.

So, let us raise our voices, united as one,
To fight against these battles, not easily won.
We stand against the wind, strong and tall,
To break down walls and tear down inequality's thrall.

Let us build a future fair for all to embrace,
Where no voice is silenced, no person misplaced.
A world where justice reigns, blessings are bestowed,
Where extreme weather and inequality are no longer bestowed.

Together, we'll weave a tapestry anew,
With compassion as our thread, and hope shining through.
For in this pursuit, a future bright shall arise,
Where extreme weather and inequality meet their demise.

So let us join hands and march forth today,
Spreading love and understanding along the way.
For only together can we truly prevail,
And create a world where justice will never fail.

Untitled
by Christian Shaw

Rusty was an old dog, he had lived with his family for many years, and every day was routine. He woke up, went down to the kitchen to eat whatever leftovers there were from breakfast, and then, he would lie down on the fluffy blue carpet in the living room, the coziest thing in the house, until noon rolled around when he could get some dinner scraps. It seems about as mundane as a dog's life could get, but not for Rusty, he was content living this way. It was only occasionally when he would talk to a little white dog named Lily from across the chain fence. Lily would tell him of all the trips her and her family go on, and Rusty would sit and listen. Rusty didn't go on vacation, in fact, he didn't go anywhere except his backyard, but like I said, Rusty was content with a mundane life.

It was windy this morning when Rusty went outside, and Lily's usual friendly face was nowhere to be seen. Her house which was usually so lively with people and noise was now dead silent. Besides this, Rusty felt an uneasiness. Rusty went through his doggy door to see his family all standing around the little TV in shock. They had lots of bags out in the living room, one of them was carrying it to the little car out front. Rusty, still uneasy, laid down on the carpet and watched as they carried the haul to the car. They all started petting Rusty, which would've been nice usually, but they were crying. Had he done something wrong? Then, he watched them all leave in the car, and Rusty laid down on the carpet to wait for them to come home.

He wasn't sure when he fell asleep, but Rusty woke up to hear the heaviest rain he had ever heard slamming against the roof. He ran to his family's room to see if they were ok, but it was dark in their room. He jumped on their bed to wake them up, but their bed was empty. Where were they? He ran to the window but to his dismay, the car was still gone. That's when he noticed it though, the street had become a river, and it was getting close to his house.

Rusty had never been so panicked in his life. Water had started dripping from his roof and seeping through the cracks in the door. It was getting close to his carpet, he grabbed it with his teeth and started pulling it away from the quickly water covered floor. The wind was getting louder, water started pouring out of the doggy door. Without realizing, Rusty dragged his carpet right into the water, watching as it began to rise along with the water. Windows shattered and wind whistled like a train horn throughout the house. Despite his compulsion to stay off the furniture, he jumped up onto the couch. What would his family think if they saw him? He had let all this water into the house, and now he was on the couch. But the water was only rising higher, and he didn't know what to do. He laid there for a minute, watching the water rise and listening to the air that only blew harder as the moments passed. Then, things began to shake, and that's when it happened, the roof flew right off of the house. Rusty was scared, he wanted to find someplace safe but he couldn't leave the house, he didn't want his family to worry about him. So he stayed on the couch, wind blowing around him, he watched the water rise still.

Despite the unrelenting elements, he began to drift off to sleep, when he was quickly awakened by a stray piece of wood flying into his chest. He was knocked over into the water, Rusty frantically paddled and pawed at the couch, but the rushing water pulled him away. He searched for anything to cling to but it was to no avail. In his final moments, Rusty's thoughts turned to his family—were they safe, and were they thinking of him too? He could only hope that they were.

Does History Really Change?
by Teigan Smith

As I sit and listen to stories from my Grandmother, my Aunts and Uncles, and my Mother, I often ask myself, "How much has history actually changed?" My grandmother often talks about the times when she was growing up and how plentiful berries would grow on vines, there were lemon trees growing, all the different neighbors who had growing vegetation in their backyards, and so much more. My aunts and uncles talked about when they played at my great-grandmother's house, how my great-grandfather would be fixing on something outside, and how the air just smelled different, the many trees that were present that you could take a nap under, being able to pick a piece of honeysuckle and get a taste while playing, and the presence of different animals passing by.

When I sit outside now, there's barely a butterfly. My mom often watches birds, but there's only a few common breeds that come to visit our yard on a daily basis. Could that be because of the extreme heat and flooding that's stifling the environment from producing? Or has history changed how families keep their yards? Do today's grandparents still plant and harvest within our neighborhoods? Has the vegetation of wild berries and honeysuckle died off because of emissions that are given off by the refineries that surround us and the many vehicles that are driven day end and day out? Or have we felt the extremes of the seasons do to human negligent behavior? I believe that the answers to these questions are all around us.

I have pictures of a watermelon patch that my grandmother was growing in her backyard, when I was at the age of 2. She loved to grow cucumbers, tomatoes, etc. My mother and my aunt still plant some things, but not nearly like my grandmother. I hear them speak about how harsh the weather has been year after year. I remember stories of where my great-grandmother lived. It was originally a marsh. Now, it has flooded in recent times, as if it is trying to return to its original state.Times have brought about a change in our environments that demand more of different things and others tend to suffer.

The Government sets many standards when it comes to environmental exposures, as they set laws for many issues within our daily lives. I don't believe we should just depend on the government, we can also make righteous decisions. The same neighborhood that I spoke about where they planted harvest amongst themselves, my aunts and uncles ate honeysuckle as they played, and witnessed the animal planet at their fingertips. Well, that same neighborhood, as beautiful as it sounds, and it was beautiful, could not live outside of those given blocks. So, again I ask myself, "Does history really change?" As I visit my grandmother, who's lived on the same land for over 60 years. My great-grandmother's land, that's well over 100 years, and the most that has changed is the neighbors have died off. Yet, the demographics haven't changed like the environment has. All the neighbors are the same like the common birds my mother sees. There's no variety, as if time just stood still in just their world. "Does history really change?" you ask. It has shown extreme changes from my great grandparents generation to mine. Weather, agriculture, and habitat changes have occurred. These are the changes, more than others.

Letters of My World's End
by Aiden Sowell

Entry 140

A storm warning was called on the island and if it hits, it's the worst storm to ever hit anywhere in the world. I believe it's fake and there's no way this possibly will hit. There's no signs of it at all and it seems to be going further north and around us. And I believe I'll be okay, especially since my family will be here with me.

I gave my family some trouble, but they have forgiven me and hopefully they'll stay. They have no reason to leave, the storm probably isn't going to hit and I'm planning on moving on working for a better self. But I still have my doubts and I know I shouldn't but some things just come to me randomly.

Am I just in denial?

That question flies through my head too much, knowing that I'm not. There's nothing to worry about. This storm is not going to happen, and my family isn't leaving.

I trust this process, and I will just trust it and pray. I just have to bring a family together and not let a storm break it apart; A long task but definitely possible. And maybe it could be better than ever before. I just have to pray and make sure it's not false hope. If it is, then I'm probably going to break. I've already had smaller incidents with the family and I was in denial then, but maybe life will finally turn around in my favor. And I could finally live in peace.

Entry 142

Well they left. And it's my fault, I know it is. They said it was the storm but it has to be me, with the trouble I've caused them I don't blame them for leaving. The words are just singeing through my brain like a needle out of a cannon. "It's for safety from the storm and for the kids." She said, with a tone that just yelled *liar!*

Now, I'm here by myself. The only place to put my thoughts is in this journal. I should be okay though, the storm isn't going to hit, and if it does, I'll survive. I'll survive just for my family, my wife, and my kids. They left because of me, and I'm going to show they shouldn't have left, and that I want to be there for them. I love them and this storm is not going to ruin that!

Remember you're only human, anger is normal.

My anger is killing and it's basically the reason I did what I did. I hurt my family due to my emotions getting the best of me.

That was my sorry excuse and I regret it now. I made them feel like they did something wrong because of my actions, I belittled them for my problems, and I chased them away due to my well-being.

Now it led to a lonely house that's too loud. Maybe they'll be back soon, but that's a tunnel dream now.

Entry 146

The storm hit, and it struck me in the worst way possible. The house is surrounded by water all around, the island is basically covered and it's too late for evacuation. Now I'm just stuck here till it passes.

The only sound I hear are the waves rushing through, carrying houses, ideas, memories and maybe lives but you'll never know. Now it's all with the water and resides in the deep, vast containment of the bellowing deep, like my soul and mind, drowning in a storm of its own. A storm contains the constant rain of failure, and the lightning adding to the mistakes of it.

Just depression, it will pass.

I say to myself, hoping that's all it really was. When I know my head is more than just demoralized and sad, it's downright insane and unhinged. I'm not correct right now and all I can do is write, pray and hope for a miracle. A miracle that this house doesn't cave in, and that my family comes back soon.

The storm itself is hard, knocking houses down everyday. This is not normal. The winds are at gliding speeds, the waves are flying through the streets, and the downpour is falling with seemingly no end. It's only a matter of time before the storm decides to beat me down, but I will be ready to take whatever comes. I've survived a storm before, and this one is going to be no different.

Entry 150

It has been about a week and the storm is already up to my house and on my first floor. I had to move up to the bedroom and put my mattress at the railings above the foyer just in case. My rations are dwindling and all I have besides that is my journal, an axe, and myself. The waves are getting louder and are at a constant flow, never ceasing to stop for anyone, including me. The rain is basically hail, falling like heavy meteors at terminal velocity.

I've been thinking to myself.

When will this bargaining be enough?

That question has been wrapping around my mind since this storm started. First it was my storm that drove my family away, and now it's driving me away. Every raindrop adds to the loneliness and desolate aura of this house, ever growing. The disparity that my life has become, compared to what it was just a few weeks ago is ridiculous. I went from a family man to a lonely dweller, just because of storms. I'm just begging for time to reverse itself, and for me to fix all of the errors and pain I've caused. I just want this pain to go, I want to find life again. Because this is not life, this is *purgatory*.

This place, which was once filled with family, memories, and life, now contains nothing more than a drained body and silence. It's on the cusp of hell, which is just pain and emptiness. I have to endure it and hope for its passing. I'm just a wishfully thinking beggar, but I'm begging I'm right and I may finally be.

Entry 156

Yes, I'm dying. There is no other way of survival for me. I have no food and water, the water is up to my second floor and still rising. I'm in my attic, sitting with my journal and nothing else. I've given up, that's all I can do. I'm trapped in here, with my brain all over the room, trying to break through for air. The house is pushing and swaying, like the thoughts of my life. I have nothing left.

Accept it. Life is over.

A thought I said to myself, realizing that this isn't me lying. This is the truth and a hurtful one. My family left because of the storm, my house was ruined by the storm, and now my life is hopeless because of the storm. It's the catalyst of my downfall! I'm trapped, lonely, lifeless, because of a storm that has little reason to exist.

The storm is my fault.

I have journal entries littering my attic floor, trying to explain how I caused this. There's just too many reasons to count. I hurt my family with force and words. I hurt myself too many times, and expected change when I didn't put effort to it. I didn't prepare well enough for the storm and I did not leave when I was supposed to. This storm is my ultimate karma for all of it, and I deserve it.

I'll accept it, as I know I should. My time has expired and I'll just face it. There's no point in hiding. The waves are here and I can feel them beating on the floor below me. They're here for me, and I have to leave life with them. This is my goodbye to the cruel world I didn't prepare for. The world that made me leave it with rigid waves, and the world I will have to leave behind.

The Winter Storm
by Avery Spell

The outside of the house was cold and wet
The people inside were not set.
They lived in the Texas heat
Not prepared for this winter's feat.
Many people huddled inside their homes
Where the coldness shook their bones.
The poor people did not have generators
Which affected them like razors.
What the poor didn't have, the rich had plenty
This hurt more than twenty.
Many froze
When it snowed.
Inequality was prevalent
This made people ambivalent.
Until the inequality is solved
Nothing will be calm.
The problem is urgent,
That is why this poem is so important.

Extreme Weather and Inequality: A Looming Crisis
by Holden Stucker

Extreme weather events, once considered sporadic occurrences, have become increasingly frequent and severe in recent years. While no one is immune to their impacts, the burden of extreme weather is not equally distributed across society. This essay delves into the intersection of extreme weather and inequality, shedding light on how marginalized communities often bear the brunt of these disasters, and why addressing this disparity is an urgent necessity.

Extreme weather events, such as hurricanes, droughts, wildfires, and floods, are on the rise due to climate change. The scientific consensus is clear: climate change is intensifying weather patterns. Consequently, the world has witnessed a surge in these events, causing immense damage to people and property.

The effects of extreme weather are far-reaching, disrupting economies and societies. Vulnerable communities face profound challenges in the aftermath of these events, including loss of life, property damage and various health and wellbeing impacts. The loss of human lives is the most tragic consequence, and impoverished areas often have limited access to life-saving resources and evacuation options. Homes, businesses, and infrastructure are frequently destroyed or damaged, leaving residents and business owners grappling with enormous financial burdens. Extreme weather events can lead to waterborne diseases, heat-related illnesses, and mental health issues, with marginalized communities having limited access to healthcare.

Extreme weather does not discriminate, but pre-existing inequalities in society magnify its impact on socioeconomic status, geographic location and a multitude of infrastructure disparities. Low-income communities lack the resources to prepare for and recover from extreme weather events. They often live in substandard housing and have fewer financial safety nets. Marginalized communities, disproportionately located in high-risk areas, are vulnerable to flooding, landslides, and other weather-related hazards. Poorly maintained infrastructure, such as inadequate drainage systems and weaker building structures, heightens vulnerability.

Inadequate preparedness and slow response magnify the suffering of governmental and institutional failures, communication gaps, and discriminatory policies. Marginalized communities frequently receive less assistance and face delays in relief and recovery efforts. Evacuation orders and safety information often fail to reach these communities effectively, leading to increased risks. Some policies unintentionally or intentionally exclude marginalized communities from receiving disaster aid.

Addressing the inequality exacerbated by extreme weather requires a multi-faceted approach which includes but is not limited to equitable preparedness, infrastructure investment, and community engagement. Governments and organizations must ensure that all communities, regardless of income or race, have access to disaster preparedness resources and information. Prioritizing the improvement of infrastructure in vulnerable areas can reduce the risks associated with extreme weather. Involving communities in disaster planning and response efforts can improve outcomes and foster resilience. Extreme weather events are a stark reminder of the urgent need to address inequality. Vulnerable communities cannot continue to bear the disproportionate burden of these disasters. Achieving a more equitable response to extreme weather requires a concerted effort from governments, organizations, and individuals to ensure that no one is left behind when the storm clouds gather. It is not just a matter of climate justice but a moral and practical imperative.

Extreme Weather in the Twin Islands of the Caribbean
by Georgia Thomson

Trinidad and Tobago, twin islands in the Caribbean, known for their picturesque beaches and hospitable people may seem like a perfect utopia, but they are no strangers to nature and extreme weather. I, a 17 year old girl, grew up in Trinidad and experienced many unfortunate weather events while living there.

Being situated within the tropical climate belt, the islands' people have learned to live with intense rainfall and occasional hurricanes, though it is challenging. These extreme events have left a mark on the islands' ecosystem, infrastructure, and lives of their people. Trinidad and Tobago has faced many tropical storms and hurricanes. These events bring heavy rainfall, strong winds, and much damage to animals, people, and their homes and businesses. One example of these devastating hurricanes is Tropical Storm Bret. Bret hit Trinidad in 2017, and remains a stark reminder of the island's vulnerability to these harsh conditions.

Hurricane Bret brought much devastation upon the islands as the storm resulted in flooding and landslides, especially in areas with poor drainage and unstable terrain. The floods and landslides displaced communities, damaged homes and habitats, and posed significant danger to residents. Several towns and cities were flooded with waters rising as high as 13 feet outside of homes. Heavy rainfall poses ultimately one of the biggest threats, not only because of flooding, and landslides, but also safety. Incident reports from after the storm claimed that one man fell to his death after slipping on a makeshift bridge while running through heavy rains.

Though Bret was short lived, there was much more damage done than just that of flooding. Roof damage was reported in approximately 100 homes, along with some downed poles and power outages. Due to strong, unbearable winds, roofs were blown off of houses, and many trees and plants were uprooted, causing them to fall and damage property. Masses of livestock and pets faced terrible conditions which they could not survive in, making the storm all that more devastating. This ultimately led to economic consequences, as a vital component of the island's economy relies on their agricultural sector. Farmers had to deal with crop damage, soil erosion, and saltwater intrusion.

The aftermath of extreme weather events in Trinidad and Tobago often leads to public health concerns. Contaminated waters can result in the spread of waterborne diseases, and the destruction of healthcare facilities can result in unfavorable outcomes, forcing residents to cope with health challenges even after the storm has cleared. Although the aftermath can be difficult, Trinidad's communities are strong and show remarkable resilience when there is a challenge like this. Trinidad and Tobago has an organization called the Office of Disaster Preparedness and Management (ODPM) which helps the people in times of need such as these. Communities come together to help each other, as well as other Caribbean islands. Government initiatives and international cooperation have played a crucial role in helping to build resilience throughout the islands.

In conclusion, I can confidently say that extreme weather may always be a challenge that my home land will face, but we will always bounce back, stronger than ever. Extreme weather events in Trinidad and Tobago, driven by tropical climate, and geographical location, have an intense impact on the lives of its people. The vulnerabilities exposed by hurricanes, floods, and landslides underscore the importance of continued efforts to improve infrastructure, enhance disaster preparedness, and promote sustainable practices. The islands' population, fabled for their strength, resilience, and adaptability, continues to work hard in the face of climate change and extreme weather patterns. Trinidad and Tobago will forever remain a beautiful place.

The Storm That Changed Everything
by Abygail Valentine

People say that rain helps you sleep
That used to be the case
I used to love the rain

August 24, 2020
It was a typical day
My friends and I were riding our bikes
Enjoying the sun
We could have never predicted what was coming

August 25, 2020
Our parents began to worry
They gave us a box
They said to pack anything you would be sad never to see again
That night, we evacuated
We knew it was coming

August 26, 2020
Two houses, 15 people, and three dogs
The adults sat by the television that night
The children were sent to bed in hopes of easing their minds
The opposite happened
I had my first panic attack
The hurricane came

August 27, 2020
The first thing we did that morning was pray
We had hope
We sat together while our mom scrolled through the pictures
Everything seemed to be okay
Until it wasn't

The first hint was when my mom started crying
I knew it was going to be bad
I went over to the phone
A 45-foot tree through the roof, the news reported
Everything stopped

I stood there in disbelief
The place where I grew up

The building that housed all of my favorite memories
All of it was gone

The next day, my parents made a decision
They were going to rent a house in Texas
This made the situation so much worse
I realized I was never going to sleep in my room again
I was never going to play in my backyard
But my emotions had to wait

The adults decided to leave the kids in Missouri
They were going back to Louisiana to do relief work
I was left with my three cousins and two siblings, all under 12
I was 14

The kids looked up to me
Every morning, I would get bombarded with questions
"Is the house going to be okay?"
"Where will we live?"
"When will mom be back to get me?"

One day, my youngest cousin found me crying
I didn't think anything of it until I later found him alone, crying in
        the bathroom
I realized that my emotions affect them
From that moment on, I put a smile on my face
I saved my feelings for my bed

I cried myself to sleep most nights
Nothing was fair
It wasn't fair that I had to pretend to be okay
It wasn't fair that I had to take care of the kids
It wasn't fair that my house was gone
But I sucked it up

I helped my aunt
I did the laundry
I cooked dinner
I washed the dishes
I made sure everyone had a nap
I grew up ten years in two days

It was August
School had started

I enrolled in a homeschool program
I tried managing the homework and taking care of everyone
I couldn't do it, I failed my classes
I unenrolled and got the kids school books
I was their teacher

The cell towers were finally fixed
I could call my mom
She told us that they were going to demolish the house
They came and got us
They needed help

We left Missouri and headed for Louisiana
I still lay awake some nights thinking of what everything looked like
      houses in rubble
My favorite ice cream shop, the place my grandpa took me after our
      special dinner dates
Completely gone
I will never forget

We spent hours packing anything we could save from our house
In the back of our minds, knowing that it would all be gone soon
I sat on the floor of my room
Letting all of the emotions I kept bottled up out
It felt like the worst day of my life

The day came
My parents wouldn't let us watch
They demolished our house
I told myself I would never go back
I would never visit the land my house used to be on

It took me three months
I finally went to see it
I got out of the car and broke
Pieces of my wallpaper were mixed in with the rocks
The memories came flooding back
My mom sat there and hugged me

The following week, I started going to a new school
I was a freshman in high school
I didn't know anyone
I refused to talk

I was so angry at the situation that I was in
I missed out on so many potential friendships
I was sabotaging myself

In my mind, there was no hope
It had been five months
I saw my siblings start to move on
I realized that I couldn't change my situation
I started to make friends
I was going to make the best out of my situation

October 14, 2023
I experienced trauma
I didn't think I would ever recover
Given the chance, I would never go back and wish for the hurricane
       to happen again
But looking back, I realize it was a blessing in disguise

Through this experience, I realized that a house is just a building
A home is the people who stand beside you
Even when situations are tough
I may have lost my house that night
But I will never lose my home

Not Flooded
by Brady Vo

The perception of good and bad weather heavily relies on an individual's unique view or idea of weather. The combination of glaring sunlight and blistering heat may be a welcome sight to some but a bane to others. Chilling winds and the sun hiding in the clouds are no different. In the same way, although it may come as a surprise to many, weather treats people with the same prejudice that it receives. As the insurance agent passed his judgement on the conditions of my childhood home, I was thrust into this devastating reality.

In Southeast Texas, the word "flood" evokes images of communities coming together to deal with the aftermath of a harsh storm. The first recollection of an event like this that I have is Hurricane Harvey. Insurance claims were made left and right, those without a home or adequate resources flocked to any assistance that nonprofit organizations offered, and other activities circulated around southeast Texas. For those in vulnerable positions after the flood, including owners of destroyed homes like my family and those without a home, forms of help were available. During the aftermath of Hurricane Harvey, I was aware of the graciousness of many that was bestowed upon me and my family. We made insurance claims to build back up the lives that we lost while staying with my aunt. However, I discovered that extreme weather did not always end in sunshine and rainbows and the storm continued for some.

The violent downpour of rain that unfolded at the commencement of my 8th-grade year came like a wolf in sheep's clothing. Nobody truly believed that the rainstorm that arrived in my hometown of Nederland, Texas would develop similarly to that of the catastrophe that had struck a couple of years prior. I went to school as normal leading up to the storm, but the Monday before the storm was when I first learned of a possible appearance of extreme weather. My English teacher informed my class that we would be receiving a lot of rain and gave the typical warning of "staying safe indoors" and being safe during the cancellation of school. My mom rolled into the school pickup line with this thought lingering in the back of my mind, but it was quickly discarded the moment I opened the car door. My mom noted that the clouds were quite dark, and I unenthusiastically and uninterestedly agreed, unaware of how important this description of the climate would be in the coming days.

I woke up to a few vibrations of my phone lying next to my head on my bedside table on the morning of the storm. I snatched my phone off the table and quickly entered my password to reveal a string of images sent by many of my friends. Videos of water creeping up to doorsteps and images of toppled-over trash cans, basketball goals, and more floating down streets saturated my feed. My first reaction to these images was to run to the front window of my house and peer through its blinds. I was not shocked to see that a comically large puddle of water was creeping up my driveway as well. I laughed awkwardly as I had no clue how to respond to such a nerve-wracking situation. I ultimately decided to place the possibility of a flooded home for the second time in two years at the back of my mind and went back to my room while darkness ensued with a region-wide power outage.

I landed on the decision that sleep was the best solution to escaping the problems of the real world with the threat of Tropical Storm Imelda at the throat of my family home. After a long slumber, I awoke to the news that the storm was dissipating when I greeted my family in the living room. My eyes widened, and I searched every corner of my house for even the slightest speck of water, but sleek tile with dry paint was all that appeared in my field of vision. A smile covered my face, and I proceeded with jubilation to my family with the belief that we had escaped the storm scot-free. I was shocked to see, though, that a dreadful mood hung over the rest of the inhabitants of my house.

I learned that a series of unfortunate events had occurred during my long sleep session. My parents had the same joy that I had upon seeing the dryness of their beloved home, but they wanted to ensure that there were no other problems. They made a quick call to someone who could inspect our house for flood damage, and he quickly came the same day after the flood in the streets had died down enough to travel on them. The moment the man arrived, as my parents recounted to me, the assessment was an easy one. There was water in our walls that had not quite made it into the house, but it was enough to prompt the action of tearing out the bottom six inches of our sheet rock and insulation. The source of my parents' dread was not this revelation, though. It was the words of the insurance agent who they called shortly after our home was assessed. My parents relayed to me exactly what the agent had said, "You can't make a claim on a home that was not actually flooded. Sorry."

My family and I were denied financial assistance because of the cruelness of the weather. It left us in purgatory, short of complete destruction but also well short of safety. The events of Hurricane Harvey repeated themselves once again at the conclusion of Tropical Storm Imelda. People received more than enough help to get back on their feet, but my family was left behind on the premise that our home had not actually flooded. The scale was tipped heavily away from us, and it took personal experience of this for me to actually realize the unfairness of natural disasters.

Although not on the far side of the spectrum, the situation of my family was still exemplary of the inequality that is born from the forces of nature. The experiences of my family not being on the extreme side shows just how many vulnerable individuals are being overlooked and overshadowed. It is important to recognize that extenuating circumstances are important to analyze, and situations are often much more complex than they initially seem.

Extreme Weather vs. Inequality

by Joshua A. Wilson

Extreme weather vs. Inequality, which is worse and why?
Here is my response, one that I will always stand by.

The harsh wind and rain, that leaves damage on the world
Or the harsh inequality, that face some boys and girls
Both cause damage, to society as a whole
But it is felt more closely, by those with lesser roles
By those who aren't of wealth, of those in the bad parts of town
Of those who don't get second looks, unless the look comes with a
    frown
However there's a difference, that I hope you will soon learn
These two are not the same, one is of greater concern
Extreme weather comes, and destroys towns in its path
But inequality destroys the lives, of those in a lower class
Extreme weather comes, and destroys the homes where we stay
But inequality destroys the lives, of people's hearts everyday
Extreme weather comes, and destroys all of our power
But inequality destroys the mistreated, all their power is devoured
Extreme weather can't be helped, it'll destroy despite our action
But inequality can be put to rest, I propose a counteraction

People can't change their looks, how they grew up, or how they were
    raised
But we can change the way we view people, don't immediately shun
    or dismay
They might be of different race, or praise a different Being
They might dress a different way, or may not be very lean
They might not be of wealth, or have fancy cars
They might not be the prettiest, nor as bright as the stars
But to just give someone a chance, despite the way they look or how
    they act
Is simple, empowering, and humble, and it is what we all lack
Because although we might be different, at our core we're all the
    same
We are all human and have a heart, that's something that will never
    change
Treat others the way you want to be treated, we've all heard that
    little chime
But let's put it into action, and destroy inequality while we still have
    time

Extreme weather vs. Inequality, which is worse and why? That was my response, one I will always stand by.

The Hurricane
by Emily Xu

When the rain came, I think I sighed,
Board the windows, stock up the candles,
No words could ever explain the way
Try to ignore the fear that washed up with the rain,
The dread, the gloom, that settled down.
Hope and pray and wish nothing happens,
The onset of the flood begins,
Hope the dog is complacent inside,
And dark, turbulent, is the sky,
Hope the neighbors are safe and dry,
As the waters, the winds, climb higher still,
Hope the weather reporter lied,
Gulping, eating, swallowing everything in its wake.
(This play is certainly a tragedy.)
The nation will never forget
Sixty-eight, all frozen in time, between life and death and the waters,
As Texas held its breath to see
The damages, the houses, the ruins,
The passing of the storm at sea.
All gone.
Sit back and try to relax
The water—
As the news, the nation,
The flood—
Gave this tempest, catastrophic storm
The winds—
An innocent name.
Harvey.
We'll never forget
That all was silent
Before the storm.

Untitled
by Molly Young

From the storm, you washed in, scared and
confused.

"From the storm," said you, "to seek refuge"

Because in that distant world you come
from, a storm comes with a price.

It's a merciless dog, biting at the heart of
your home.

Watch as it drags it away, while you watch,
weeping.

Weeping just as the rain you stand in, your
life being torn from you.

From the storm, you seek refuge.

From the storm, hope is destroyed.

Dreams of college, replaced by wishes for
a roof over your head.

Visions of stardom now fading, you sleep
under the stars every night.

From the storm, you seek refuge.

From the storm, you seek what was taken.

Lovely Weather
by Treyquinn Young

In a world of extremes, where weather does rage,
Inequality's grip takes center stage.
From melting ice caps to scorching heat waves,
Mother Nature's fury, humanity craves.

But amidst the chaos, a story unfolds,
Of inequality, stark and bold.
For while some bask in comfort and wealth,
Others battle hardships, their struggles felt.

The hurricane's wrath may spare the elite,
But the impoverished face nature's deceit.
Their homes destroyed, their lives upended,
They fight for survival, their voices blended.

As floodwaters rise and droughts persist,
The privileged watch from their lofty mist.
A tale of two worlds, stark and contrasting,
Leaving the marginalized forever fasting.

Oh, how cruel the winds of inequality blow,
Causing suffering that few truly know.
But we must unite, against this unjust tide,
And fight for justice side by side.

For weather extremes are but a reflection,
Of societal flaws and our own disconnection.
Let us stand together, and voices raise,
To mend the broken, deserving of praise.

In this battle against both nature and man,
We'll rise above, with a united plan.
To bridge the gap, to heal the divide,
And create a world where equality can abide.

So let us strive, with passion and might,
To bring an end to this unequal fight.
For in our hands lies the power to change,
And build a future where fairness will reign.